T0016882

3 MINUTES *with* Jesus

3 MINUTES *with* Jesus

180 Devotions for Men

TRACY SUMNER

Print ISBN 978-1-63609-576-9

Published by Barbour Publishing, Inc., 1810 Barbour Drive, Uhrichsville, Ohio 44683, www.barbourbooks.com

Our mission is to inspire the world with the life-changing message of the Bible.

Printed in China.

INTRODUCTION

Focusing on Jesus is the perfect way to spend time each day. He is your Savior, your Lord, and your Teacher—and He wants you to spend time with Him each day.

This book is a collection of moments that help you meet with Jesus, get to know Him better, and strengthen your walk with Him. Within these pages you'll be guided through just-right-size readings you can finish in as few as three minutes:

- Minute 1: Reflect on Jesus' own words or scripture readings about Him
- Minute 2: Read real-life application and encouragement
- Minute 3: Pray

These devotions aren't meant to be a replacement for digging deep into the scriptures or for personal, in-depth quiet time with Jesus. Instead, consider them a great jump-start to help you form a habit of spending time getting to know Jesus better every day. Or add them to the time you're already spending with Him. Share these moments with friends, family, coworkers, and others you come in contact with every day. They're looking for inspiration and encouragement too.

Jesus Christ is the same yesterday, today, and forever.

HEBREWS 13:8 NLT

THE ETERNAL JESUS

In the beginning was the Word, and the Word was with God, and the Word was God. He was with God in the beginning.

John 1:1–2 niv

Since the very beginning when God created the cosmos, many billions of people have lived here on this little blue planet we call home. Out of those billions of souls, Jesus was truly one of a kind.

Each of us humans was a created being—except for one. The Bible teaches that Jesus, the second person of the Trinity, was with God for eternity past. He is the Son of God, God in the flesh, and the one our loving heavenly Father sent to earth to live a sinless life and then die a sacrificial death so that we could enjoy eternity in heaven with God.

Jesus, the more I think about the truth of who You really are, the more I'm astounded at Your love for me. You didn't have to leave Your eternal home in heaven, but You chose to come to earth to live as a man and then die for me so that I could live forever in heaven with You.

I AM: THE BREAD OF LIFE

Jesus said to them, "I am the bread of life; whoever comes to me shall not hunger, and whoever believes in me shall never thirst."

John 6:35 ESV

Speaking to a big crowd gathered on the shores of the Sea of Galilee, Jesus spoke this promise: "Blessed are those who hunger and thirst for righteousness, for they will be filled" (Matthew 5:6 NIV).

Jesus had come to earth to minister to spiritually hungry and thirsty people; and in John 6:35, He identified Himself as "the bread of life," meaning that He alone would be the spiritual nourishment each man so desperately needs.

The people following Jesus that day knew that God had provided their ancestors with manna (bread) to keep them from starving. Every one of those ancestors eventually died, but Jesus told His listeners, "But here is the bread that comes down from heaven, which anyone may eat and not die" (John 6:50 NIV).

When you feel spiritually hungry and thirsty, run to Jesus for satisfaction.

Dear Jesus, only You can satisfy my spiritual hunger and thirst. May I turn to You alone when I feel that inner hunger and thirst.

I AM: THE LIGHT OF THE WORLD

Again Jesus spoke to them, saying, "I am the light of the world. Whoever follows me will not walk in darkness, but will have the light of life."

JOHN 8:12 ESV

We live in a world shrouded in terrible spiritual death and darkness. Most men have no hope of getting themselves on the track God intended for them. No hope, that is, but Jesus!

Jesus self-identified as "the light of the world," meaning He is the one source of spiritual light. Jesus wanted His listeners to understand that they didn't have to live lives of hopelessness, darkness, and slavery to sin. Instead, if they would simply believe in and follow Him, He would give them the transforming, restoring "light of life."

Decades after Jesus had returned to heaven, the apostle John wrote, "If we walk in the light, as he is in the light. . .the blood of Jesus, his Son, purifies us from all sin" (1 John 1:7 NIV).

You live in a dark, lost world. But Jesus has promised to give you light.

Thank You, Jesus, that I can walk in Your light every minute of every day.

I AM: THE DOOR

"I am the door. If anyone enters by me, he will be saved and will go in and out and find pasture."
JOHN 10:9 ESV

Many people today truly believe that men can find their way to peace with their Creator through any number of ways. *As long as someone is sincere in their beliefs, God is good with that*, they believe.

But that is not what God says in the Bible.

When Jesus said, "I am the door," He was stating clearly that He was the only way for a man to receive God's forgiveness and to enter into His eternal kingdom. In John 10:8 (NIV), Jesus referred to those who choose to follow Him as "sheep," saying, "All who have come before me are thieves and robbers, but the sheep have not listened to them."

There is no other door to eternal life except through Jesus. That is the simple message He calls each of us to believe and proclaim.

Jesus, give me the courage to lift You up as the one and only way to peace with God and to life eternal with God in heaven.

I AM: THE GOOD SHEPHERD

"I am the good shepherd. The good shepherd lays down his life for the sheep."
John 10:11 ESV

Centuries before Jesus came to earth, David wrote Psalm 23 (NIV), which begins, "The Lord is my shepherd, I lack nothing." When Jesus said, "I am the good shepherd," He identified Himself as the one David depended on for care, provision, and protection.

People who lived in the land of Israel while Jesus was on earth understood the relationship between shepherds and sheep. They knew that shepherds provided sheep safety, protection, food, and water. Without the shepherd watching over and caring for the flock, the sheep stood little chance of surviving for long. They would either be carried away by hungry predators or die of hunger and thirst.

The same is true for us today. We need Jesus' love and care. Without it, we have no chance of surviving spiritually. With it, we can live victoriously.

Jesus, thank You for being my good shepherd. May I always trust You enough to follow You and depend on You for safety, provision, and restoration for my soul.

I AM: THE RESURRECTION AND THE LIFE

Jesus said to her, "I am the resurrection and the life. The one who believes in me will live, even though they die; and whoever lives by believing in me will never die."

John 11:25–26 NIV

Jesus spoke His words in John 11:25–26 to a grieving woman named Martha, whose brother Lazarus had died four days prior. Martha believed that her brother would one day be raised from the dead, but Jesus was about to show her that He had power over death that very day and forever.

Jesus stepped to the mouth of the tomb and called out, "Lazarus, come forth!" Moments later Lazarus came out into the daylight. Martha and her sister didn't have to wait to be with their brother again. But more importantly, Jesus, the man who had just called Himself "the resurrection and the life," showed that death was no obstacle for Him.

Jesus is the one and only source of resurrection and eternal life. Without Him, we have neither; but with Him, we will one day be raised from the dead and will have everlasting life.

Jesus, thank You for being my source of everlasting life.

I AM: THE WAY AND THE TRUTH AND THE LIFE

Jesus answered, "I am the way and the truth and the life. No one comes to the Father except through me."

John 14:6 NIV

In John 14:6, Jesus made perhaps His most powerful statement concerning who He really was and what it means to each of us today. Jesus was and is:

The Way: Jesus isn't just a way to God's forgiveness and salvation—He is the one and *only* way. God has communicated very clearly in His written Word that there is only one sacrifice acceptable to Him for the forgiveness of sin—His one and only Son.

The Truth: You've probably heard it said that each man needs to find his own truth. But in John 14:6, Jesus stated clearly that He is God's truth itself.

The Life: Jesus alone is the source of life—both life on this earth and eternal life in God's kingdom.

Jesus is the way and the truth and the life. He truly is everything we need!

Thank You, Jesus, for being the way to peace with God and for being my source of eternal truth and life.

I AM: THE TRUE VINE

"I am the true vine, and my Father is the gardener."
John 15:1 niv

Jesus wanted His disciples to understand that He didn't expect them to do any of the great things He had called them to do under their own power. In John 15:5 (niv) He told them, "I am the vine; you are the branches. If you remain in me and I in you, you will bear much fruit; apart from me you can do nothing."

The wonderful truth Jesus stated to His closest followers applies to us today as well. If we want to live the lives God wants us to live and do for Him and His kingdom the things He has called us to do we'll need to remain in close fellowship with Jesus every day. Otherwise, we can do nothing of eternal value for Him.

Jesus, thank You for being my vine. Remind me often to cling to You and depend on You daily so that I can do the things You've called me to do.

A BLESSED CONFESSION

Whoever confesses that Jesus is the Son of God, God abides in him, and he in God.

1 John 4:15 ESV

God the Father sent Jesus, His one and only Son, to rescue us from a prison—the prison of sin and separation from Him—we could never have escaped from on our own. He didn't have to do it, but He willingly, even joyfully, sent the very best He had so we could have everlasting life in the very presence of God.

We must never forget—and never stop confessing—that Jesus was more than God's representative, more than God's spokesman... He is the very Son of God, the second person of the Trinity (Father, Son, and Holy Spirit), God in the flesh. And when we know Him in a personal, intimate way, He gives us the ability to confess with our mouths who He really is.

Lord Jesus Christ, thank You for making it possible for me to have renewed fellowship with the Father and He with me. Thank You for taking the punishment I deserve for my sins.

JESUS' MISSION STATEMENT

"For I have come down from heaven, not to do my own will but the will of him who sent me."

John 6:38 esv

A mission statement is defined as a formal summary of the aims and values of a company, organization, or individual. In John 6:38, Jesus issued a mission statement of sorts when He stated that He had come to earth not to do His own will but the will of His Father in heaven.

The apostle Paul wrote of Jesus' earthly mission: "He made himself nothing by taking the very nature of a servant, being made in human likeness. And being found in appearance as a man, he humbled himself by becoming obedient to death—even death on a cross!" (Philippians 2:7–8 niv).

Jesus was so committed to the Father's will that at the moment of truth, when He faced a horrific death for our sins, He prayed from His heart, "Not my will, but yours be done" (Luke 22:42 niv).

That's what perfect commitment to God's will looks like!

Lord Jesus, thank You for obeying Your heavenly Father by dying in my place so I could be at eternal peace with God.

THE FORGIVEN SHOULD FORGIVE

"For if you forgive other people when they sin against you, your heavenly Father will also forgive you."
MATTHEW 6:14 NIV

If you're honest with yourself, you would have to admit that it's not always easy to have a heart attitude of forgiveness toward some people. But that's exactly what Jesus calls you to do.

Forgiveness is a big deal to God, so big that He sent Jesus to earth to sacrifice Himself so He could forgive us for our sins. And Jesus taught that this God of forgiveness requires His people to forgive others when they say and do things that hurt or offend us.

God wants to make you more and more like Jesus every day. And when you choose to forgive others for the wrongs they have done against you, you do what Jesus did for you.

Lord Jesus, You did what no one else could do when You made a way for me to be forgiven for even my worst sins. Thank You! Remind me often that You want me to forgive those who have hurt or insulted me, even when they don't deserve it.

TAKING UP OUR CROSS

"And whoever does not take his cross and follow me is not worthy of me."
MATTHEW 10:38 ESV

Jesus never promised His followers an easy path in this life. In fact, He challenged us to "take [our] cross" and follow Him every day. Jesus' followers during His earthly ministry would have understood that the challenge He issued in Matthew 10:38 was not a call to an easy life. On the contrary, it was a call to difficulties.

Jesus calls every professing Christian man to deny himself and follow Him. That means willingly putting our own desires, our own personal dreams, and our own agendas aside and following and loving Jesus with our whole heart. This is a 100 percent commitment to Jesus and what He wants for us. It isn't an easy commitment to make, but it comes with the promise of amazing eternal rewards.

Jesus, You never promised that being Your disciple would be easy. Strengthen me so I can take up my own cross each day and follow You with everything I have.

TRUSTING JESUS' TEACHING

So Jesus answered them, "My teaching is not mine, but his who sent me."
JOHN 7:16 ESV

Many people who don't know or follow Jesus acknowledge that He was a great teacher who directed men in how to live a better, happier life—a life that benefits themselves and others alike.

Jesus was indeed a great teacher, but His ability to speak life-changing words into the lives of His followers was yet further proof of who He really was—the Son of God.

In John 7:16, Jesus deflected attention away from Himself and toward His heavenly Father, in effect telling people that His amazing teaching wasn't the result of His own studies or credentials. Every word of His teaching, He said, came straight from the God who had sent Him to earth.

You can fully trust Jesus' wisdom and teaching because it comes straight from God Himself.

Lord Jesus, Your teaching comes straight from God in heaven. That means that I can completely trust everything You have said to me and others who follow You.

HE PRAYS FOR YOU!

Consequently, he is able to save to the uttermost those who draw near to God through him, since he always lives to make intercession for them.

HEBREWS 7:25 ESV

In His "High Priestly Prayer," Jesus prayed for all who would believe in Him after He returned to heaven (see John 17:20–24). But in Hebrews 7:25, the author of the book of Hebrews promises that Jesus "lives to make intercession" for those who have come to God through Him.

What an amazing promise! The same Jesus who bridges the eternally wide gulf between us sinful humans and a holy God also stands in the gap for us today, offering prayers for us—prayers pleading for our forgiveness and prayers pleading for God's blessings on us.

Everything Jesus said and did while He was on earth was to glorify God and benefit us. As we face life's struggles and temptations, Jesus sits at the right hand of God, asking that He comfort and strengthen us to face everything this life throws our way.

Jesus, thank You for seeing my struggles and temptations and for taking them straight to Your heavenly Father in prayer.

BE SANCTIFIED!

"Sanctify them by the truth; your word is truth."
John 17:17 niv

In his first letter to the Thessalonian church, Paul wrote, "For this is the will of God, your sanctification" (1 Thessalonians 4:3 esv). In the New Testament, the word *sanctify* means being set apart from this world for God's pleasure and purposes.

Just before Jesus was arrested, tried, and crucified, He prayed for His disciples, "Sanctify them by the truth." Jesus was asking His Father in heaven to set them—and us—aside for His very own purposes.

In John 17:17, Jesus stated, "Your word is truth." Taken as a whole, this verse means that God will sanctify us when we read, learn, and apply God's Word in our lives.

Sanctification takes time and work—the work God does in us through His written Word, the Bible. That is God's will—and also what Jesus asked Him to do for us today.

Lord Jesus, thank You for beginning the work of setting me aside for God's purposes. Help me to do my part in that process by spending time in Your written Word every day.

IT'S ALL POSSIBLE WITH GOD

Jesus looked at them and said, "With man this is impossible, but not with God; all things are possible with God."

Mark 10:27 NIV

Jesus shook up His disciples when He said, "How hard it is to enter the kingdom of God! It is easier for a camel to go through the eye of a needle than for someone who is rich to enter the kingdom of God" (Mark 10:24–25 NIV).

"Who then can be saved?" they asked one another (Mark 10:26 NIV).

Jesus told them the simple truth about salvation for anyone, including the rich: without God it's impossible, but with God *all things* are possible.

This world presents all sorts of distractions that can keep men from truly seeking God: money, power, popularity, and many others. It's easy for us to look at those who are fully invested in those things and think they are hopelessly far from the Lord.

But when you start believing that someone is beyond hope, remember Jesus' words: *"All things are possible with God."*

Jesus, may I never think of anyone—no matter how far he or she is from You—as beyond Your reach.

ONE WAY ONLY

For there is one God and one mediator
between God and humanity, Christ Jesus,
Himself human, who gave Himself—a ransom
for all, a testimony at the proper time.

1 Timothy 2:5–6 HCSB

In 1 Timothy 2:5–6, Paul echoed the words of the Lord Jesus when He said, "I am the way and the truth and the life. No one comes to the Father except through me" (John 14:6 NIV).

This is the Bible's message, and it's hardly one that today's world would see as "inclusive." Modern thinking believes a man can take any road to God, as long as he follows it with sincerity and conviction. But the Bible teaches that sincerity and conviction are not enough.

Holding unflinchingly to the biblical message that Jesus is the one and only way to eternal salvation can lead to moments of discomfort. You may be called "narrow-minded" or "bigoted"—and you may lose relationships for speaking the message.

But cling to that message and speak it for as long as God gives you breath. It's the message this world desperately needs to hear.

Jesus, may I always boldly speak the truth that
You are the one and only way to salvation.

OUR PERFECT ROLE MODEL

Live a life filled with love, following the example of Christ. He loved us and offered himself as a sacrifice for us, a pleasing aroma to God.

EPHESIANS 5:2 NLT

Jesus once told His closest followers, "I have set you an example that you should do as I have done for you" (John 13:15 NIV). Ephesians 5:2 contains essentially the same message, encouraging us to "live a life filled with love."

As those who follow Jesus, we are commanded to be imitators of our heavenly Father who sent us the perfect example of love in the person of His one and only Son. Jesus sacrificed Himself on the cross for us, but He also set an example of love in His every word and action.

We, as Christians, are to be imitators of our Father. We do that by looking to Jesus, the one who is "the image of the invisible God" (Colossians 1:15 NIV).

Jesus, may I always follow Your example of love. You loved me and sacrificed Yourself for me, and You want me to love others the same way.

MUSTARD SEED FAITH

"You don't have enough faith," Jesus told them. "I tell you the truth, if you had faith even as small as a mustard seed, you could say to this mountain, 'Move from here to there,' and it would move. Nothing would be impossible."

MATTHEW 17:20 NLT

As Jesus—with His three closest disciples following along—returned to the other disciples, He found that they had failed in their attempts to cast a stubborn evil spirit out of a young boy. After Jesus healed the boy, the disciples asked Him why they couldn't cast the demon out.

Jesus scolded the disciples for their lack of faith and told them that all it took was just a very small amount of faith—as small as a mustard seed—to move mountains for the kingdom of God.

When you place your faith—even if it is very small—in our mighty God, nothing will be impossible for you.

Jesus, help me to remember that the size of my faith isn't nearly as important as where I put that faith. May my faith be 100 percent in You.

SEEING THE FATHER

Jesus answered: "Don't you know me, Philip, even after I have been among you such a long time? Anyone who has seen me has seen the Father. How can you say, 'Show us the Father'? Don't you believe that I am in the Father, and that the Father is in me?"

JOHN 14:9–10 NIV

Philip, one of Jesus' twelve disciples, had followed Jesus for three years. He had listened to His heart-changing wisdom and teaching, witnessed His amazing miracles, and seen in Him a man of perfect character.

Yet the truth of who Jesus really was hadn't fully penetrated Philip's heart and mind. "Lord," Philip said, "show us the Father and that will be enough for us" (John 14:8 NIV).

Jesus gently but firmly scolded Philip for his lack of understanding, telling him, "Anyone who has seen me has seen the Father. . . . Don't you believe that I am in the Father, and that the Father is in me?"

Jesus came to earth so you could know God as your loving heavenly Father, so you can know His heart and His thoughts toward you.

Lord Jesus, thank You that knowing You means knowing God the Father.

A FRIEND OF SINNERS

When Jesus heard this, He told them, "Those who are well don't need a doctor, but the sick do need one. I didn't come to call the righteous, but sinners."

MARK 2:17 HCSB

After calling a tax collector named Levi (also known as Matthew) to follow Him, Jesus went to this notorious sinner's home for dinner with him. . .and many other notorious sinners.

When the Jewish religious leaders of that time witnessed Jesus dining with these lost souls, they were indignant. But as Mark 2:17 suggests, Jesus was right where He was needed and being what He had come to earth to be: a friend of sinners.

Jesus never consorted with sinners or joined with them in their sin. But He associated with them and befriended them, showing them the love and compassion they so desperately needed.

Do you consider yourself a friend of sinners—the kind of friend Jesus was to those who needed Him?

Jesus, help me to be a friend of sinners—the kind who shows them love and compassion and who gently leads them into Your truth.

HUMILITY

"So anyone who becomes as humble as this little child is the greatest in the Kingdom of Heaven. And anyone who welcomes a little child like this on my behalf is welcoming me."

MATTHEW 18:4–5 NLT

Jesus was more than a little piqued when His disciples blocked people from bringing their small children to Him so He could bless them. He used their error to teach them an important lesson about faith.

Jesus used the children as an object lesson about the kind of faith God requires from each of us. The kind of faith God honors, Jesus taught them, is a childlike faith. It's a faith that comes to Him with an open heart and an open hand, with a simple trust, and with an expectation that He wants to do good for those who come to Him.

How would you describe your faith in God today? In what ways do you think it needs to change?

Father in heaven, help me to come to You daily with childlike faith—trusting, helpless, openhearted, and fully dependent on You for everything.

BE READY!

*In your hearts honor Christ the Lord as holy,
always being prepared to make a defense to anyone
who asks you for a reason for the hope that is
in you; yet do it with gentleness and respect.*

1 Peter 3:15 esv

Before He departed earth to return to His Father in heaven, Jesus assigned His disciples the task of taking the message of salvation to the world around them. Jesus had done amazing things in these men's lives, and He wanted them to share what they knew and what they had with many others.

Today, Jesus calls you to do the very same thing.

The Lord has done amazing things for you—starting with saving you and preparing a place for you in heaven. He also gave you His Holy Spirit, who helps you to live a Christlike life and who empowers you to share your faith with others.

As a follower of Jesus, people should see evidence in your life of what He has done for you. Knowing that should motivate you to always be ready to gently speak the promise of salvation through Him.

Jesus, help me to be ready when I have an opportunity to introduce You to others.

DON'T BE AFRAID!

When they saw Him walking on the sea, they thought it was a ghost and cried out; for they all saw Him and were terrified. Immediately He spoke with them and said, "Have courage! It is I. Don't be afraid."

MARK 6:49–50 HCSB

Talk about a rough night! Jesus had sent the disciples away, commanding them to board their boat and cross the Sea of Galilee while He stayed behind to pray. But a powerful headwind pushed relentlessly at their boat, making for slow going on their way toward the far shore.

The disciples must have wondered if things would be different for them had Jesus been there with them. But Jesus knew of His followers' struggles, and He arrived on the scene—walking on the water! Jesus boarded the boat, and immediately the wind died down.

When you find yourself struggling against the headwinds of life, remember that Jesus sees and cares—and that He'll never leave you alone to live in futility.

Jesus, I know I'll face sometimes-frightening headwinds of life. But when You are with me, I know I don't have to give in to debilitating fear. Keep my eyes on You always.

THE PERFECT LAMB OF GOD

The next day John saw Jesus coming toward him and said, "Look! The Lamb of God who takes away the sin of the world!"
John 1:29 NLT

When John the Baptist saw Jesus approaching him, he made a public declaration of Jesus' true identity when he called Him "the Lamb of God who takes away the sin of the world!" John understood that God had sent Jesus to earth to be the perfect sacrifice for our sin.

In Old Testament times God required His people to sacrifice flawless lambs so their sins could be forgiven. But God had a perfect plan to replace these once-a-year sacrifices with a perfect, one-time sacrifice for our sins.

Jesus lived a perfectly sinless life here on earth (see Hebrews 4:15). But one day He would die a horrible, violent death so we could be forgiven and then live forever with Him in heaven.

So thank Jesus every day. . .for who He is and what He has done for you.

Dear Jesus, thank You for being the perfect, sinless Lamb of God. You are the only one who could take away my sin. Thank You for giving Your life for me.

FREE INDEED!

"So if the Son sets you free, you will be free indeed."
JOHN 8:36 ESV

The Bible teaches that every person is born under what the apostle Paul called "the law of sin and death." That means we are all born spiritually dead because of our sin. It means we are in bondage to sin—in a prison from which we have no way to escape.

But Jesus came to rescue us and to free us from the eternal ravages of sin. That is what Paul was pointing to when he wrote, "Because through Christ Jesus the law of the Spirit who gives life has set you free from the law of sin and death" (Romans 8:2 NIV). And it's what Jesus meant when He said, "If the Son sets you free, you will be free indeed."

Freedom is always better than slavery, and eternal life is better than eternal death. And Jesus died for you so you can have freedom and eternal life.

Thank You, Jesus, for setting me free from the law of sin and death. You have made me free, so I can rejoice that I am free indeed!

WHAT HE ENDURED

Looking to Jesus, the founder and perfecter of our faith, who for the joy that was set before him endured the cross, despising the shame, and is seated at the right hand of the throne of God.

HEBREWS 12:2 ESV

Though Jesus suffered unimaginable physical and spiritual agony on a wooden cross nearly two thousand years ago, He never complained or pled His case with His tormentors. Instead, He remained focused on His ultimate purpose for coming to earth—to surrender Himself as a perfect sacrifice for our sin.

This is not just an example of God's amazing love, but also the greatest act of love in all of human history. God's only Son, an innocent man who was condemned to die, endured the shame of false accusations, blasphemous mocking, brutal beatings, the crown of thorns, and being hung on a cross for everyone to see. He could have called down a legion of angels to rescue Him, but He endured—simply because of His commitment to God's plan... and because of His love for those who would know Him as their Lord and Savior.

Jesus, thank You for enduring the pain and humiliation of the cross—for me.

FORGIVING WITHOUT LIMITS

Then Peter came to him and asked, "Lord, how often should I forgive someone who sins against me? Seven times?" "No, not seven times," Jesus replied, "but seventy times seven!"

MATTHEW 18:21–22 NLT

Peter probably thought he had impressed Jesus when he asked Him if he should forgive someone who had sinned against him up to seven times. Forgiving someone seven different times is certainly a good thing. But the twelve disciples were astonished when Jesus said to forgive others "seventy times seven" times.

That's 490 times! they probably thought. *He can't really mean this!*

But Jesus meant it. He was calling His followers to a life marked by unlimited forgiveness for others, a life well defined by these words from the apostle Paul: "Be kind and compassionate to one another, forgiving each other, just as in Christ God forgave you" (Ephesians 4:32 NIV).

So forgive others who hurt or offend you—and not just 490 times, but as many times as necessary.

Jesus, You have forgiven me for more acts of sin and rebellion than I can possibly count. May I always forgive others, even when they offend or hurt me many times over.

LIVING A "GOLDEN" LIFE

"Do to others as you would have them do to you."
LUKE 6:31 NIV

Think about some of the things you like others to do for you. Do you like hearing kind words of encouragement? Do you like it when someone comes through for you in a pinch—say when you need help moving or painting your home? Is it important to you to have others stand by you during difficult times? If you answered yes to any of the above questions, then you would do well to follow Jesus' words in Luke 6:31, also known as "the Golden Rule."

It's not always easy to treat people with kindness or to do good to them. Some are just difficult to love. If you find yourself struggling to do good for others, remember that Jesus did the kindest, most loving thing in all of history when He died for you. When He did that, He set an example for you to follow every day.

Jesus, help me to always do for others the same things I'd like them to do for me.

RESCUED!

He has rescued us from the domain of darkness and transferred us into the kingdom of the Son He loves. We have redemption, the forgiveness of sins, in Him.

Colossians 1:13–14 HCSB

Before the fall of man (see Genesis 3), humans lived in the light of God's goodness and love. But after Adam and Eve chose sin over obedience, this world has become what Colossians 1:13 calls "the domain of darkness." This is the realm of the devil himself, and he has enjoyed dominion over the world's systems, which he uses to deceive and destroy humankind, God's most prized creation.

But Colossians 1:13–14 also delivers the wonderful news that Jesus has "rescued us from the domain of darkness and transferred us into the kingdom of the Son."

What an amazing exchange!

Jesus defeated the devil and his works on the cross—and one day He will bring us into His eternal kingdom. . .and put Satan in his place for all eternity.

Jesus, thank You for rescuing me from Satan's domain of darkness and transferring me into the eternal kingdom of God.

THE SOURCE OF ABUNDANT LIFE

"The thief comes only to steal and kill and destroy. I came that they may have life and have it abundantly."

JOHN 10:10 ESV

When most men think of the word *abundant*, their minds go to abundant possessions, abundant money, abundant prestige, and other sources of temporal happiness this world offers. But when Jesus promised those who follow Him "abundant life," He wasn't talking about any of those things.

In the New Testament, abundance means exceedingly, beyond measure, a quantity considerably greater than we should expect. When Jesus used the word *abundantly*, He was talking about those things He promises to do within us, starting at the very moment we turn to Him for salvation.

Our part in receiving that abundant life is to follow Jesus' command: "Remain in me, as I also remain in you. No branch can bear fruit by itself; it must remain in the vine. Neither can you bear fruit unless you remain in me" (John 15:4 NIV).

Jesus, I want the abundant life You promised. Help me to focus not on material or financial abundance but on the spiritual abundance the Bible says I have in You.

PERSECUTION: EXPECT IT!

In fact, all those who want to live a godly life in Christ Jesus will be persecuted.

2 Timothy 3:12 HCSB

In today's scripture verse, Paul makes Christians a promise most of us probably wish we could just overlook. Yes, we want to "live a godly life in Christ Jesus," but we'd just as soon skip the persecution part.

But we can trust Paul when he says we'll be persecuted for living godly lives. After all, Paul knew about these things (see 2 Timothy 3:11).

In modern-day America, Christians don't face the kind of persecution Paul suffered for Jesus' sake. Mostly, we endure negative comments—sometimes outright untruths—for being followers of Christ.

But no matter what form of persecution you face, you can rest in this promise from the mouth of Jesus: "God blesses you when people mock you and persecute you and lie about you and say all sorts of evil things against you because you are my followers" (Matthew 5:11 NLT).

Jesus, when I am criticized or mocked for following You, help me to remember that God blesses those who face all sorts of persecution.

SERVING OTHERS FIRST

Sitting down, He called the Twelve and said to them, "If anyone wants to be first, he must be last of all and servant of all."

MARK 9:35 HCSB

Jesus knew that His disciples had been arguing among themselves, and He knew what they were arguing about. It was time for a sit-down.

Jesus knew what was going on, but still He asked them, "What were you arguing about on the way?" (Mark 9:33 HCSB). Hearing no answer, Jesus told them, "If anyone wants to be first, he must be last of all and servant of all."

Being "last of all" doesn't mean you aren't important or useful to God. It simply means you consistently treat others like they are more important than you are. It means serving in any way you can and sharing what you have with people you know are in need. It means encouraging those who need encouragement.

Do you want to be great in God's kingdom? Then always make it your goal to put others ahead of yourself.

Lord Jesus, help me to always remember that You want me to put others ahead of myself and care for others every day.

RECONCILED

All this is from God, who reconciled us to himself through Christ and gave us the ministry of reconciliation: that God was reconciling the world to himself in Christ, not counting people's sins against them. And he has committed to us the message of reconciliation.

2 Corinthians 5:18–19 niv

All men are estranged from God and without hope of being reconciled to Him—without hope, that is, if it weren't for God so graciously bringing us to Himself through His Son, Jesus Christ. God so loved humanity that He initiated what 2 Corinthians 5:18–19 calls "the ministry of reconciliation."

God would have been 100 percent justified had He simply abandoned all people to an eternity apart from Him in a terrible place called hell. Instead, He brought us to Himself through Jesus—because He *wanted* to.

Having reconciled us to Himself through Jesus Christ, God now desires that we take part in His ministry of reconciliation by telling others about Jesus and what He has done for them.

Lord Jesus, thank You for reconciling me to God through giving Yourself as the perfect sacrifice for my sins. I want to serve You by speaking Your message of reconciliation to others.

BELIEVING AND RECEIVING

I ask you again, does God give you the Holy Spirit and work miracles among you because you obey the law? Of course not! It is because you believe the message you heard about Christ.

GALATIANS 3:5 NLT

Many men tend to believe that receiving something means we have done something to "earn" it. But the Bible teaches something completely different when it comes to receiving God's Holy Spirit.

No man has ever received God's Spirit or seen His power working in his life by simply "willing" it to happen. That only happens when we believe in our hearts the simple message of Jesus Christ.

Do you ever find yourself trying to make God act on your behalf by "doing" things you believe will earn His favor? If so, stop! Instead, simply believe, and then receive all He has for you.

Generous heavenly Father, remind me daily that Your gift of the Holy Spirit comes only because I believe what You and Your only Son have said in Your written Word.

FULL MEMBERS OF GOD'S FAMILY

So now you Gentiles are no longer strangers and foreigners. You are citizens along with all of God's holy people. You are members of God's family.

Ephesians 2:19 NLT

God worked through His chosen people—the nation of Israel—to bless every nation by bringing the Messiah, Jesus Christ, into the world. In Ephesians 2:19, the apostle Paul—himself a Jewish man—tells non-Jewish (Gentile) Christians that they are "no longer strangers and foreigners" but full citizens of His kingdom and members of His eternal family.

What a blessing God has conferred upon us all—including those who were not born into His chosen nation of Israel! As full members of God's family through Jesus Christ, we have full access to Him as His own beloved people. We are, as Peter wrote, "a chosen people, a royal priesthood, a holy nation, God's special possession, that you may declare the praises of him who called you out of darkness into his wonderful light" (1 Peter 2:9 NIV).

Lord Jesus, I was once a stranger to God, but no longer. Thank You for making it possible for me to be welcomed into God's eternal family.

GAINING RIGHTEOUSNESS

I do not set aside the grace of God, for if righteousness could be gained through the law, Christ died for nothing!

GALATIANS 2:21 NIV

We, as men, often judge ourselves and others based on performance. If good things happen to us, then it follows that we must have done something to deserve it. Our own performance truly does matter in many ways in this world. But the Bible teaches that God accepts us and declares us righteous not because of our own performance and rule-keeping but because of *grace.*

In Galatians 2:21, the apostle Paul wrote that if we could gain God's righteousness through keeping the law, then Jesus' death on the cross means nothing. Paul also wrote, "For it is by grace you have been saved, through faith—and this is not from yourselves, it is the gift of God—not by works, so that no one can boast" (Ephesians 2:8–9 NIV).

God's grace. . .it truly is amazing!

Lord Jesus, change my heart and guide my steps. May I focus my eyes on You and not on my own performance.

A CALLING MISSED

Jesus told him, "If you want to be perfect,
go and sell all your possessions and give the
money to the poor, and you will have treasure
in heaven. Then come, follow me."

Matthew 19:21 NLT

The wealthy young man was by most standards a good person who kept God's commandments all his life. But something was missing. Jesus told him that he needed to unburden himself of his earthly wealth and follow Him.

This young man walked away from Jesus and returned to his life of wealth and ease. Missing out on what Jesus offered him made him sad, but he just couldn't rid himself of the one thing that kept him from being a true disciple. He had learned what it took to be a member of God's kingdom, but he couldn't—or wouldn't—do what Jesus required of him.

Today's world offers many distractions that can, if not put in their proper place, keep us from following Jesus with our whole heart. What is Jesus calling you to give up for Him today?

Jesus, please reveal to me anything that keeps me from following You with my whole heart, 100 percent of the time.

YOUR NUMBER ONE FOCUS

"But seek first his kingdom and his righteousness, and all these things will be given to you as well."
MATTHEW 6:33 NIV

Each man has responsibilities here on earth. It's not wrong for you to concern yourself with caring for yourself and your family. In fact, God calls you to do just that. God put these people in your life, and He wants you to love them and care for them.

But they should not be your life's top priority.

God wants you to put all things behind your relationship with Him. So don't let anything, even your most pressing needs and responsibilities, take your focus off the God who loves you so much that He sent Jesus to give His life for you. When you put the Lord and His kingdom first, He'll take care of everything else.

Jesus, You have promised that my Father in heaven will give me everything I need to live my life for You here on earth. Help me to focus first on You and Your kingdom and not on my needs, knowing that You have those things covered.

PREACHING THE GOSPEL

Then He said to them, "Go into all the world and preach the gospel to the whole creation."
MARK 16:15 HCSB

In Mark 16:15, Jesus spoke to His disciples about "the Great Commission." This was Jesus' "marching orders" to take His message of salvation to the world around them after He returned to heaven.

You may already know this, but Jesus' call to preach the gospel applies to His followers today. That means you have the privilege—and the responsibility—to tell people in your sphere of influence about how they can have peace with God and eternal life through Jesus.

You don't have to be a missionary, pastor, or evangelist to be qualified to tell others about salvation through Jesus. Just ask God to guide you toward people who need to hear about Him, and to prepare your heart to speak up when He gives you the opportunity to speak His name.

Savior Jesus, I want to help others to know You as I know You. Help me to keep my eyes and ears open for opportunities to "preach the gospel."

THE FOREMOST OF SINNERS

The saying is trustworthy and deserving of full acceptance, that Christ Jesus came into the world to save sinners, of whom I am the foremost. But I received mercy for this reason, that in me, as the foremost, Jesus Christ might display his perfect patience as an example to those who were to believe in him for eternal life.

1 TIMOTHY 1:15–16 ESV

When the apostle Paul called himself "the foremost" of sinners, he wasn't speaking out of false humility. Paul knew that God had forgiven him for a long list of horrendous sins—namely, the deaths and imprisonments of the Christians he had so terribly persecuted before he met Jesus on the road to Damascus (see Acts 9:1–9).

Paul's conversion, as well as the wonderful work he did in preaching the gospel of Jesus afterward, shows us two things about God's nature. First, He sometimes uses the most unlikely (humanly speaking) characters to do great works for Him. Second, it shows us that no one, even the worst of sinners, is beyond God's reach.

Jesus, help me to remember that no one is beyond Your reach, that no one is a lost cause.

A HIGH PRIEST WHO UNDERSTANDS

For we do not have a high priest who is unable to empathize with our weaknesses, but we have one who has been tempted in every way, just as we are—yet he did not sin.

HEBREWS 4:15 NIV

Do you ever feel completely alone? You need someone to talk to, someone who understands your faith struggles, your temptations, and your battles in the mind. When you feel that way (and we all do at times), Hebrews 4:15 says you have a Savior who truly "gets you."

When you face times of trouble, when your faith is waning, or when you feel overwhelming temptation, the writer of Hebrews says you can turn to your High Priest, Jesus: "Let us then approach God's throne of grace with confidence, so that we may receive mercy and find grace to help us in our time of need" (Hebrews 4:16 NIV).

You're truly never alone!

High Priest Jesus, thank You for being a Savior I can talk to, a Savior who understands me and my struggles and weaknesses. I have You, so I never have to struggle alone.

WHEN JESUS BECAME SIN

And about the ninth hour Jesus cried with a loud voice, saying, "Eli, Eli, lama sabachthani?"—that is to say, "My God, My God, why have You forsaken Me?"

Matthew 27:46 skjv

Jesus endured unimaginable pain and suffering during the hours of His arrest, trial, torture, and crucifixion. But for Him, the absolute worst moment came when He was—for the first time ever—separated from His Father in heaven.

On the cross, Jesus cried out, "My God, My God, why have You forsaken Me?" God had made Jesus, "who had no sin to be sin for us, so that in him we might become the righteousness of God" (2 Corinthians 5:21 niv). At that moment, a holy God, who cannot look on sin, could do nothing but look away from His beloved Son.

The Bible teaches that there is always a price to be paid for sin; and when God poured out His wrath on His Son, that terrible price was paid. And Jesus paid that price all alone. . .for you and for all who would follow Him.

Jesus, never let me forget the things You suffered—especially separation from Your heavenly Father—for me.

WASHED BY JESUS

"No," Peter protested, "you will never ever wash my feet!" Jesus replied, "Unless I wash you, you won't belong to me." Simon Peter exclaimed, "Then wash my hands and head as well, Lord, not just my feet!"

John 13:8–9 NLT

Peter probably thought he was demonstrating true humility when he told Jesus, "You will never ever wash my feet!" But Jesus quickly set Peter straight, telling him that unless He washed the disciple, he wouldn't belong to Him. Peter got the message—a message that applies to us today.

The apostle Paul listed sins that will bar people from God's eternal kingdom (1 Corinthians 6:9–11). But he went on to proclaim to the Corinthian Christians, "But you were washed. . .in the name of the Lord Jesus Christ and by the Spirit of our God" (1 Corinthians 6:11 NIV).

Jesus washing His disciples' feet was a powerful example of our Lord's humility. But it also shows us that in order for us to connect with Him in a meaningful, eternal way, we need Him to clean us from the inside out.

Thank You, Jesus, for doing for me what I could never do for myself—cleansing me so I can one day inherit the kingdom of God.

BE MERCIFUL

"Be merciful, just as your Father is merciful."
LUKE 6:36 NIV

Jesus' command in Luke 6:36 isn't the easiest one to obey consistently.

Mercy is important to God, so important that He gave the very best He had—His Son, Jesus—to live as a man and die a terrible death so He could pour out mercy on us. It's also important to Him that we show mercy to others, even when they don't deserve it. . .*especially* when they don't deserve it!

The bottom line is that when we show mercy, especially when it's not deserved, we demonstrate a heart of obedience to the Lord, we do our part to be at peace with others, and we show gratitude to the God who forgives and freely and willingly showers us with mercy whenever we mess up.

Father, thank You for being merciful to me. On my own, I can't be as merciful to others as You call me to be. Strengthen me and soften my heart so I can obey Jesus' call for me to be merciful, just as You are merciful.

REAL LOVE

By this we know love, that he laid down his life for us, and we ought to lay down our lives for the brothers.

1 John 3:16 ESV

There are many different definitions of the word *love*. There is romantic love—the kind a man feels for the woman who is the object of his affection. There is familial love, which has as its object our wife, kids, and other family members. And there is brotherly love, which we have for friends we care about.

"Love," as it appears in 1 John 3:16, is a love that never changes and never demands anything in return. It is a love demonstrated even toward the unlovable and toward those who reject it. It is a love we show others, not just in what we say but in our actions.

That is the kind of love Jesus demonstrated when He died on the cross for us. And it's the same love we are to have for others.

Jesus, help me to love others the way You loved me. May my love be undying, unconditional, and displayed not just in my words but in my actions.

BORN AGAIN

Jesus replied, "Very truly I tell you, no one can see the kingdom of God unless they are born again."

John 3:3 NIV

Nicodemus, a Pharisee who went out of his way to meet with Jesus, couldn't quite grasp what Jesus meant when He told him a person must be "born again" before he could see the kingdom of God.

The phrase "born again" means "born from above." It is a new birth in which God takes someone who is spiritually dead and makes him spiritually alive and transforms him and changes his eternal destiny. The apostle Paul summarized this process when he wrote that God "made us alive with Christ even when we were dead in transgressions" (Ephesians 2:5 NIV).

Jesus performed many amazing miracles when He was here on earth. But His greatest miracle is making spiritually dead sinners alive so they can live forever with Him.

Thank You, Jesus, for giving me the gift of eternal life simply because I believe and trust in You. Thank You for the spiritual birth You have worked in my heart and for the growth You work within me.

BROUGHT NEAR

But now you have been united with Christ Jesus. Once you were far away from God, but now you have been brought near to him through the blood of Christ.

EPHESIANS 2:13 NLT

When we read that we "were [once] far away from God," we wouldn't be wrong to think we were once *infinitely* far away from Him.

Before he knows Jesus, a man is without fellowship with God, without an eternal home in heaven, without access of any kind to God's throne, and without hope of doing anything about the sin that created an absolutely eternal separation from the Lord.

But Paul also wrote that a man who has been "united with Christ Jesus" has been "brought near to [God] through the blood of Christ."

Our sin had created an impenetrable barrier between ourselves and God. But Jesus' shed blood removed that barrier and has given us full access to our loving heavenly Father.

Thank You, Lord Jesus, for shedding Your blood so I could be brought near to my Creator and enjoy intimate fellowship with Him.

GOD'S WORDS OF APPROVAL

When all the people were being baptized, Jesus was baptized too. And as he was praying, heaven was opened and the Holy Spirit descended on him in bodily form like a dove. And a voice came from heaven: "You are my Son, whom I love; with you I am well pleased."

LUKE 3:21–22 NIV

What an amazing scene! All three members of the Trinity—the Father, the Son, and the Holy Spirit—appeared on the scene at Jesus' baptism in the Jordan River. As Jesus came up out of the water, the Holy Spirit descended on Him and the Father's voice thundered from heaven, declaring, "You are my Son, whom I love; with you I am well pleased."

At this moment Jesus received the empowerment of the Holy Spirit and the verbal approval of God Almighty for the ministry He was about to undertake here on earth. From that moment forward everything Jesus did and said pointed to His ultimate mission—to die on the cross so God could say of us, "You are my son, whom I love; with you I am well pleased."

Lord Jesus, thank You for following the Father's plan to provide salvation to all who believe and trust You.

REAL TEMPTATION

Jesus, full of the Holy Spirit, left the Jordan and was led by the Spirit into the wilderness, where for forty days he was tempted by the devil. He ate nothing during those days, and at the end of them he was hungry.

Luke 4:1–2 NIV

Jesus had just been at the spiritual mountaintop—His baptism, where He received God's verbal seal of approval. The Holy Spirit was leading Him into a literal wilderness where the devil would severely tempt Him to abandon God's plan.

But why would God the Father allow Jesus to be tempted? Was there some purpose for this chapter in our Savior's life on earth? The writer of the book of Hebrews says Jesus was tempted so He could better identify with the sinners He came to save: "For we do not have a high priest who is unable to empathize with our weaknesses, but we have one who has been tempted in every way, just as we are—yet he did not sin" (Hebrews 4:15 NIV).

Jesus, thank You for facing down temptation so You could complete Your mission to save sinners like me.

IT IS WRITTEN. . .

But he answered, "It is written, 'Man shall not live by bread alone, but by every word that comes from the mouth of God.'"

MATTHEW 4:4 ESV

Satan no doubt believed he had Jesus right where he wanted Him. Jesus hadn't eaten in forty days, and His body was in desperate need of nourishment. So the devil sidled up to Jesus and suggested that He turn some stones into bread (see Matthew 4:3). But Jesus refused, simply because He had come to serve others, not Himself—and turning stones to bread was not part of God's plan.

The devil tempted Jesus three times, and each time Jesus responded by quoting the Word of God (see Matthew 4:4, 7, 10). In doing that He set an example we can all follow when we are tempted to sin. Rather than argue with the devil, Jesus simply answered, "It is written. . ."

We, too, can resist temptation by answering Satan's lies with the truth of God's Word.

Thank You, Jesus, for showing me how I can resist the devil when he tries to tempt me into sinning against You.

A MATTER OF THE HEART

"You have heard that it was said, 'You shall not commit adultery.' But I tell you that anyone who looks at a woman lustfully has already committed adultery with her in his heart."

MATTHEW 5:27–28 NIV

In Matthew 5:27–28, Jesus quoted God's seventh commandment—"You shall not commit adultery" (Exodus 20:14 NIV). In Old Testament times, God had forbidden sexual activity with anyone other than a person's spouse, and that commandment still stands today. But Jesus took this prohibition to a different level, teaching that it isn't just about where we take our bodies but (even more importantly) about the impure places our hearts and minds can go so easily.

Avoiding lust in today's sex-saturated world is no easy task. Sometimes it seems as though every other image that comes across our field of view has the potential to cause us problems. For men today, it's a matter of commitment. . .to our spouses, our children, and our walk with Jesus.

Dear Jesus, help me to keep my heart pure from lust and my eyes away from those things that take my mind to impure places.

PRAYER AND FAITH

"I tell you the truth, if you have faith and don't doubt, you can do things like this and much more. You can even say to this mountain, 'May you be lifted up and thrown into the sea,' and it will happen. You can pray for anything, and if you have faith, you will receive it."

MATTHEW 21:21–22 NLT

Jesus' disciples looked with amazement at a withered fig tree that only moments before had been a lush, beautiful plant. "How did the fig tree wither so quickly?" they asked (Matthew 21:20 NLT). Jesus explained that this miracle was the result of His prayer of faith that the tree would no longer bear fruit. He then encouraged them to have that same kind of faith.

This account shows us two things about prayer: First, it must be offered in faith, and second, it must be in agreement with God's will. When Jesus cursed the fig tree, He knew it would die. Also, He knew it was His Father's will that He use the dead fig tree to teach His disciples an important lesson about the relationship between faith and answered prayer.

Jesus, thank You for teaching Your disciples, including me, about the importance of faith when I pray.

GOD'S SERVANT

Behold my servant, whom I uphold; mine elect, in whom my soul delighteth; I have put my spirit upon him: he shall bring forth judgment to the Gentiles.

ISAIAH 42:1 KJV

Centuries before Jesus came to earth, the prophet Isaiah used the term "servant" to describe the coming Messiah. Later the apostle Matthew wrote that Jesus had fulfilled the prophecy in Isaiah 42 (see Matthew 12:17–21).

Jesus once told His followers that He wanted them to serve one another (see Matthew 20:24–27). He concluded this thought by telling them they should follow His example: "Just as the Son of Man did not come to be served, but to serve, and to give his life as a ransom for many" (Matthew 20:28 NIV).

Indeed Jesus came to earth to serve God and humanity by suffering, dying on a cross, and then rising from the dead. He served us in the most profound way possible, and now He calls us to serve others just as He served us.

Lord, help me to serve others as You have served me.

REST FOR YOUR SOUL

"Come to me, all you who are weary and burdened,
and I will give you rest. Take my yoke upon you
and learn from me, for I am gentle and humble
in heart, and you will find rest for your souls.
For my yoke is easy and my burden is light."

MATTHEW 11:28–30 NIV

Jesus once used the analogy "My yoke is easy" as He encouraged people to come to Him for rest. Jesus was speaking to people who had been burdened by a legalistic system of works laid on them by Jewish religious leaders of the day.

Today, our burdens don't necessarily come from legalistic religious teaching, but they are our burdens nonetheless. Jesus' promises to the people of His time still apply to us today.

Sometimes it seems like we can't find rest for our weary souls. But when the burdens of life become too heavy for you to bear, you can find rest and peace by yoking yourself to Jesus and His amazing teaching.

Jesus, today I choose to remove all my burdens from my shoulders and place them on Yours and rest in You and receive Your peace.

A MATTER OF TRUST

Jesus answered, "The work of God is this: to believe in the one he has sent."
John 6:29 NIV

John 6:28 (NIV) contains an important and well-intentioned question that many ask today—one that a group of Jesus' followers asked Him: "What must we do to do the works God requires?"

The crowd was no doubt expecting Jesus to speak a list of rules and specific assignments. But the people were probably surprised when He gave them this simple, wonderful answer: *Trust in Me!*

Jesus calls men today to a heart attitude of unflinching trust in Him. It is through trust that we are saved, and it is through trust that we are able to do anything of value for the kingdom of God. In short, Jesus calls us above all else to trust Him. When we do that, we can do the things that please Him.

Lord Jesus, I trust You as my Savior. Help me to continue trusting You more and more every day so I can be and do what pleases You.

ONE IN JESUS!

There is neither Jew nor Gentile, neither slave nor free, nor is there male and female, for you are all one in Christ Jesus.

GALATIANS 3:28 NIV

In the many years since Paul wrote the words of Galations 3:28, many have interpreted them to mean that God had done away with all differences between people groups. But God didn't do anything of the sort! Paul's message was simply this: anyone from any people group who comes to faith in Jesus is now bound together as one with every other believer in a wonderful group God calls the body of Christ.

That's a heart-bind that will last for all eternity!

God doesn't call us Christians to ignore or discount our individual differences or uniqueness. He created those differences! Instead He wants us to make sure we never allow those differences to keep us from focusing on what binds our hearts together forever—that we are truly "one in Christ Jesus."

Thank You, Jesus, that despite our many differences as human beings, we can see ourselves as one in You.

MOTIVATED BY LOVE

Therefore, my friends, I want you to know that through Jesus the forgiveness of sins is proclaimed to you. Through him everyone who believes is set free from every sin, a justification you were not able to obtain under the law of Moses.

Acts 13:38–39 NIV

God chose and prepared Paul, a man who had viciously persecuted the first generation of Christians before he had a miraculous encounter with Christ, to become a great ambassador for Jesus. During his first missionary journey (see Acts 13–14), Paul hit the ground running, preaching to his fellow Jews and Gentiles alike about Jesus' power to save.

In a place called Pisidian Antioch, Paul fearlessly spoke the gospel message in the city's synagogue. Though God had set Paul on a course far different than the one he had been on, he still loved his fellow Jews and wanted them to know Jesus. He loved them enough that he preached what he knew was an unpopular message of justification through Jesus.

Like Paul we should let love motivate us to fearlessly and consistently speak the truth.

Lord Jesus, help me to love others enough to tell them Your truth.

STRENGTHENED BY GOD'S GRACE

You then, my child, be strengthened by
the grace that is in Christ Jesus.
2 Timothy 2:1 ESV

Timothy, a young protégé of the apostle Paul and the leader of a church in the deeply pagan city of Ephesus, needed help and strength to effectively carry out his many responsibilities. In his second letter to Timothy, Paul told Timothy where to get that strength and help.

"You then, my child," Paul wrote, "be strengthened by the grace that is in Christ Jesus." Paul wanted his young friend to understand that he was not to draw on his own inner strength but to rely on God's grace given freely to those who trust in Jesus Christ.

It can be tempting to think God wants us to develop our own inner strength and rely on our own abilities and gifts. But He wants us to rely solely on the power He has made available to us through Jesus.

Dear Jesus, forgive me for trying to live my life and follow You under my own power. May I always rely on the strength You have promised to give me.

HE'S ALIVE!

And the angel answered and said unto the women, Fear not ye: for I know that ye seek Jesus, which was crucified. He is not here: for he is risen, as he said. Come, see the place where the Lord lay.

MATTHEW 28:5–6 KJV

Jesus had told His disciples at least three times that He would be crucified but that God would raise Him from the dead three days later. But they didn't understand what He meant, and on the day He was raised, some faithful women who had followed Him were the first to learn He was not in His tomb. Jesus was alive!

The Bible tells other stories of people who had been raised from the dead—including the son of a widow (1 Kings 17:17–24), the Shunammite woman's son (2 Kings 4:18–36), and Jesus' friend Lazarus (John 11:38–44)—but each of these people eventually died again. It was different with Jesus. After God raised Him from the dead, He bodily returned to heaven to live forever at His Father's right hand.

Jesus is alive today—and because He's alive, you can live forever.

Jesus, praise Your name. You are alive today and forever!

OVERFLOWING GRACE

But the gift is not like the trespass. For if the many died by the trespass of the one man, how much more did God's grace and the gift that came by the grace of the one man, Jesus Christ, overflow to the many!

Romans 5:15 niv

When Adam sinned against God, he brought about the curse of death for all of humanity. His one transgression—that one act of disobedience—brought a death sentence to every human being born into this world. Even the very best of men are born into sin and God's condemnation.

A 100 percent holy and 100 percent perfect God would be justified in consigning every human to eternal death. But this all-holy, all-perfect God is also a God of love and mercy, and because of His amazing grace, we can be saved through the work of the one perfect man who ever lived—Jesus Christ, God's Son, who came to earth to save sinners from certain death.

Jesus, I don't deserve God's love or mercy. But because He is a God of grace, I will spend eternity in heaven with You.

A TIME OF TESTING

[Jesus] said to Philip, "Where shall we buy bread for these people to eat?" He asked this only to test him, for he already had in mind what he was going to do.

John 6:5–6 NIV

Jesus was about to perform one of His greatest miracles—the feeding of five thousand hungry people—but before He did, He took the time to teach His disciples an important lesson.

Jesus knew what He was going to do, but He asked Philip how they could possibly buy enough food to feed such a large crowd. Philip answered, "It would take more than half a year's wages to buy enough bread for each one to have a bite!" (John 6:7 NIV).

Philip's problem was that he was focused on the problem at hand when the solution was right in front of him. Had Philip been fully in tune with Jesus, he would have answered, "I don't know how we can feed these people, but You do. Tell me what You want me to do."

When God asks you to do something that is beyond your means, you can ask the same question.

Jesus, thank You for providing the means I need to do what You want me to do.

GOD'S GIFT OF LIFE

But God is so rich in mercy, and he loved us so much,
that even though we were dead because of our sins,
he gave us life when he raised Christ from the dead.
(It is only by God's grace that you have been saved!)

Ephesians 2:4–5 NLT

Before we came to Christ for salvation, each of us was completely spiritually dead because of our sins. Spiritually dead people have nothing to offer, they aren't capable of loving God, and they have no chance of entering His eternal kingdom after they die.

But there is hope for all people, for God's infinite love and compassion motivated Him to provide a way for the spiritually dead to have life. He did that when He sent His Son to die for us and then be raised from the dead so we could be made alive in Him.

Never forget, your salvation has *nothing* to do with anything good in you and *everything* to do with God's goodness and love.

Thank You, Jesus, that the Father in heaven loved me, a man who was dead in my sins. That is what God's amazing grace is all about!

GOD'S LOVE FOR THE HELPLESS

For while we were still helpless, at the appointed moment, Christ died for the ungodly.
ROMANS 5:6 HCSB

As men we don't like to think of ourselves as helpless. We like to think that no matter how dire our circumstances are, we can find a way to work things out. The Bible, however, teaches that when it comes to our sin and its consequences, we are helpless—lost in the darkness of our sin and unable to find a way out.

Romans 5:6 shows us the greatness of the love of God, who sent Jesus to die for ungodly people—people who in and of themselves are undeserving and unlovable.

What an amazing act of love and mercy!

When you think of how hopeless and helpless you are without Jesus, you can't help but praise God and thank Him for loving you so deeply that He gave His only Son to die for you.

Jesus, I know that without You I am helpless and without hope. But You came at God's appointed time to die for me and rescue me from the consequences of my sin.

FISHERS OF MEN

And he said to them, "Follow me,
and I will make you fishers of men."
MATTHEW 4:19 ESV

At the very moment Jesus called the brothers Peter and Andrew to follow Him, He let them know that their life focus would change. Following Jesus often means leaving certain things behind to pursue something far grander. In this case, Peter and Andrew would be leaving a life of fishing for a life of bringing others to Jesus.

The brothers would spend the next three years following Jesus everywhere He went—witnessing His miracles and listening to His world-shaking teaching. And when those three years were over, they were ready to do the work He had called them to do when He first said to them, "Follow me."

Matthew's Gospel reports, "At once they left their nets and followed him" (4:20 NIV). In doing that, Peter and Andrew set an example for all disciples of Christ: follow Jesus.

Jesus, I know You want me to be a "fisher of men."
Grant me the courage to speak up and tell others
about You and everything You have done for me.

LOVING AS JESUS LOVES

"A new commandment I give to you, that you love one another: just as I have loved you, you also are to love one another."

John 13:34 ESV

Jesus had just demonstrated His servant heart and His love for His disciples by washing their feet (John 13:1–20). After sending His betrayer Judas away, He gave them a "new" commandment: "Love one another: just as I have loved you, you also are to love one another."

Jesus had taught the disciples much about loving others and about loving God. But this commandment was different. They were to love as Jesus loved.

Jesus had just spent three years loving the disciples—sacrificially, humbly, honestly—and now He wanted them to know how important it was that they love one another the same way.

Jesus' words made a lasting impression on the disciple John, as they should on us, for decades later he wrote, "Dear friends, let us love one another, for love comes from God" (1 John 4:7 NIV).

Lord Jesus, help me to love my brothers and sisters in You the way You have loved me.

AN ETERNAL HOME

"There is more than enough room in my Father's home. If this were not so, would I have told you that I am going to prepare a place for you? When everything is ready, I will come and get you, so that you will always be with me where I am."

JOHN 14:2–3 NLT

The disciples did not grasp the heartache they would suffer in the coming hours, but Jesus did. He was preparing Himself for the agony of the cross—and for His glorious return to heaven to be with His Father.

Jesus wanted to give the disciples some desperately needed hope, so He promised them—and us—that His return to heaven would include preparation for the day when He would welcome them to their home in heaven where they would be with Him for all eternity.

Because of what Jesus has done for us, we will one day go home to be with God!

Dear Jesus, I look forward to the day when You return and take me to my eternal home in heaven. Thank You for preparing a place for me in God's eternal kingdom.

HE IS RISEN!

[Jesus] was delivered over to death for our sins
and was raised to life for our justification.
Romans 4:25 NIV

Jesus' death on the cross is the moment when God provided the once-and-for-all sacrifice for our sin. But in Romans 4:25, Paul states that while Jesus died for our sins, He was also raised from the dead three days later, making it possible for us to be made right (justified) with God.

Paul also stated this truth more strongly when he wrote, "And if Christ has not been raised, our preaching is useless and so is your faith. . . . And if Christ has not been raised, your faith is futile; you are still in your sins" (1 Corinthians 15:14, 17 NIV).

So when you pray and thank God that Jesus died for your sins, don't forget to also thank Him from your heart for the empty tomb. Because He lives, you will live with Him forever!

Jesus, my heart is full of joy when I think about the wonderful truth that God raised You from the dead so I can live forever.

GIVING IN FAITH

And my God will supply all your needs according to His riches in glory in Christ Jesus.

PHILIPPIANS 4:19 HCSB

The Christians living in Philippi were far from financially rich, but they gave sacrificially and joyfully, knowing their contributions would help the apostle Paul in his efforts to take the message of salvation through Jesus into the surrounding world.

The Philippians set a fine example of sacrificial giving, and they also received a message from Paul essentially stating, "You are in poverty, but you have helped me. Because you have been so generous, God will meet all your needs from His riches in glory in Christ Jesus."

Perhaps God has been speaking to your heart about giving to a ministry committed to reaching people for Jesus. If you are worried that giving may put you in financial straits, remember God's promise to the Philippians—and then give as He directs you.

Lord Jesus, help me to give generously—even sacrificially—to the work others are doing to take the message of salvation through Jesus into the world.

"WEARING" JESUS

Clothe yourself with the presence of the Lord Jesus Christ. And don't let yourself think about ways to indulge your evil desires.
ROMANS 13:14 NLT

It has been said many times that "the clothes make the man." How you choose to dress can affect how you behave in certain situations.

The apostle Paul used clothing in a figurative way in Romans 13:14 as he encouraged us to "clothe yourself with the presence of the Lord Jesus Christ." That's a word picture that describes how a man can show the world around him the goodness, the glory, and the work of Jesus in his life.

Jesus should be our spiritual clothing—and when He is, we will focus on representing Him and not on ways to satisfy our own desires.

When you get up in the morning, it's important that you dress appropriately. But it's far more important that you "clothe yourself" in Jesus!

My Savior, may I always cover myself in Your wonderful presence every moment of every day.

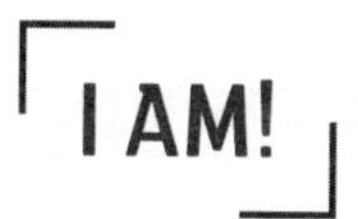

I AM!

"Very truly I tell you," Jesus answered, "before Abraham was born, I am!"

JOHN 8:58 NIV

Jesus enraged a group of Jewish religious leaders who had asked Him how He could possibly have seen Abraham. Jesus answered, "Before Abraham was born, I am!"

These Pharisees knew that God had identified Himself to Moses as "I AM" (see Exodus 3:14), and they understood that Jesus was claiming to be the eternal God incarnate, because they took up stones to kill Him (John 8:59).

It can be easy sometimes to lose sight—if only momentarily—of who Jesus really is. Some see Him as a good man and a great teacher who spoke with uncommon wisdom. Others see Him as a representative of God—a prophet. Jesus was and is those things, but He is so much more. He is God in the flesh, who lived in eternity past and will live on in eternity future.

He is the Great I Am!

Lord Jesus, help me to always remember and honor You for who You really are—the eternal God incarnate who came to earth to rescue a sinner like me.

VICTORY OVER SIN AND DEATH

The sting of death is sin, and the power of sin is the law. But thanks be to God! He gives us the victory through our Lord Jesus Christ.

1 Corinthians 15:56–57 niv

When Adam and Eve chose sin over perfect fellowship with their loving Creator, they brought death and destruction into what had been a perfect creation and into the human experience. Worse yet, their sin brought separation between a holy God and His most prized creation.

But God had a plan to reconcile sinful humanity back to Himself. Almost immediately after Adam and Eve sinned, God announced He would send a Savior into the world to defeat sin and death once and for all.

When Jesus died and was raised from the dead, He broke the power of sin, death, and the law for everyone who would believe in Him. We have victory in the Lord Jesus Christ and eternal life in a forever home with Him in heaven.

Thank You, Jesus, for defeating the power of sin and death and for giving me eternal life in heaven.

HEARING THE SHEPHERD'S VOICE

"My sheep listen to my voice; I know them, and they follow me."

JOHN 10:27 NIV

On a few occasions, Jesus likened His followers to sheep following their Shepherd. In today's scripture verse, He spoke of His sheep listening for His voice and choosing to follow Him.

If you've ever had a pet dog, you know that dogs respond most attentively to their owner's voice. Your dog just seems to understand that you are the source of everything they need and want—food, water, shelter, protection, and (of course) love and affection. Likewise, sheep need nourishment, water, protection, and a nice pasture to rest in. Because the shepherd provides those things, the sheep learn to follow when they hear his voice.

We believers first heard Jesus when we began our lives in Him—and as time goes on we become more familiar with His voice as we spend time reading scripture and praying. And as we hear His voice, we follow Him more and more closely each day.

Jesus, I thank You that I have heard Your voice—and can continue hearing Your voice every day so I can always follow You, my Good Shepherd.

SECURE IN JESUS' HANDS

"I give [my sheep] eternal life, and they shall never perish; no one will snatch them out of my hand. My Father, who has given them to me, is greater than all; no one can snatch them out of my Father's hand."

John 10:28–29 niv

There are wonderful benefits to following Jesus, our Good Shepherd, starting with His gift of eternal life. Though our lives here on earth will eventually end, our lives in heaven with Jesus will last forever. To paraphrase a beautiful old hymn, after we've been in God's eternal paradise for ten thousand years, we have no fewer days there than when we first entered it.

Jesus also said that nothing and no one will ever snatch us out of His hand. The Good Shepherd will always care for His sheep and protect them. Though we will go through severe testing in this life, we are always safe and secure in His hands.

Thank You, Jesus, that I can be secure in You and in the knowledge that You have given me the greatest gift of all: eternal life in heaven with You.

FULFILLING THE LAW

"Do not think that I have come to abolish the Law or the Prophets; I have not come to abolish them but to fulfill them."

MATTHEW 5:17 ESV

In the New Testament, the term "the law" refers to the rules and regulations God gave to the nation of Israel through Moses. The Bible teaches that the law could not provide eternal salvation but was God's means to reveal humankind's sinfulness.

Only one man—Jesus—perfectly kept every single requirement of God's holy law. He never sinned against His Father in heaven in any way, making Him the spotless Lamb of God who alone could save us through His sacrifice on the cross.

When Jesus said, "I have not come to abolish [the Law or the Prophets] but to fulfill them," He was pointing to the blessed truth that He would fulfill the demands of the law on behalf of everyone who trusted Him for their eternal salvation.

Lord Jesus, You were the only man ever to have perfectly obeyed the law of God. In doing that, You showed Yourself as the only one who could fulfill the demands of the law on my behalf.

IN JESUS' NAME

"You can ask for anything in my name, and I will do it, so that the Son can bring glory to the Father."

JOHN 14:13 NLT

You've probably noticed that most prayers in church services, Bible studies, and other gatherings end this way: *In Jesus' name, amen!* In John 14:13, Jesus encouraged His followers to make their prayer requests to God *in His name*. . .and *He will do it*.

Praying in Jesus' name is a good thing, but it's important to pay attention to the purpose of this promise: "So that the Son can bring glory to the Father."

Jesus never promised to give us everything we want when we pray in His name. Instead, He promises to do what we ask but only when it glorifies God. So before you bring your requests to God in Jesus' name, search your heart and ask yourself, "Does this request glorify God?" If the answer is yes, then ask. . .in Jesus' name!

Dear Jesus, thank You for giving me access to the Father so I can make my requests known to Him. May all my requests be for those things that glorify God.

BLESSINGS FOR THE "POOR"

"Blessed are the poor in spirit, for theirs is the kingdom of heaven."

MATTHEW 5:3 NIV

Today's scripture verse covers the first of eight "beatitudes"—meaning "statements of blessing"—Jesus spoke in the Sermon on the Mount in Matthew's Gospel. He began the sermon by stating that the "poor in spirit" are blessed because the kingdom of heaven belonged to them.

The phrase "poor in spirit" means spiritual poverty. The poor in spirit are those who understand that they have nothing of value to offer to God and that they are spiritually bankrupt before Him. They approach a holy but loving God as beggars with empty hands outstretched in hopes of receiving from Him.

We men don't like the thought of admitting we are poor and needy. But Jesus promises that when we humble ourselves and admit how little we have to offer God, we will receive eternal life in the kingdom of heaven.

Jesus, I have nothing to offer You but what You've given me. Thank You for giving me the best You have—simply because I humbly come to You with outstretched hands.

IN MOURNING

"God blesses those who mourn,
for they will be comforted."
Matthew 5:4 NLT

In what is called the parable of the Pharisee and the tax collector, Jesus contrasted the words and heart attitudes of those who had gone to the temple to pray. The Pharisee, a powerful Jewish religious leader, boasted of his own piety, reminding God how he had lived a more righteous life than most and had consistently tithed. But when the tax collector, a notorious sinner, prayed, he couldn't even lift his eyes toward heaven. Instead, he simply pounded his chest and cried out, "God, have mercy on me, a sinner" (Luke 18:13 NIV).

Only one of those two men left the temple justified before God, Jesus said, and it wasn't the Pharisee!

The tax collector stands as an example of a man who came to God with a mournful attitude over his own sin. And he's also an example of a man God comforted—the very way Jesus promised He would in the second beatitude.

Jesus, thank You for helping me to mourn over my own sinfulness. Thank You, too, for comforting and forgiving me.

MEEK, NOT WEAK

"Blessed are the meek, for they will inherit the earth."
MATTHEW 5:5 NIV

Jesus once held Himself up as an example of humility when He said, "Take my yoke upon you, and learn of me; for I am meek and lowly in heart" (Matthew 11:29 KJV).

Though the two words sound a lot alike, *meek* and *weak* have very different meanings. Weakness means lacking power, while meekness means humility, both toward God and toward other people. It speaks to having power but using it only for the benefit of others. It means being like Jesus, "who, being in very nature God, did not consider equality with God something to be used to his own advantage; rather, he made himself nothing by taking the very nature of a servant, being made in human likeness" (Philippians 2:6–7 NIV).

Jesus perfectly modeled meekness during His time here on earth, making Him the perfect example to follow for those who want to receive God's blessings.

Lord Jesus, help me to grow strong and courageous in my walk of faith in You. Help me also to be a humble man, just like You were when You lived and ministered here on earth.

HUNGERING AND THIRSTING FOR RIGHTEOUSNESS

"Blessed are those who hunger and thirst for righteousness, for they will be filled."
MATTHEW 5:6 NIV

We, as men, can have a hunger and thirst for many things—more money, more power, more success, more happiness. . .the list goes on and on. We often try to satisfy ourselves through any number of worldly means. But in Matthew 5:6, Jesus tells us we are truly blessed when we hunger and thirst for God's righteousness.

Jesus identified Himself as the only one through whom our hunger and thirst for righteousness can be satisfied: "I am the bread of life; whoever comes to me shall not hunger, and whoever believes in me shall never thirst" (John 6:35 ESV).

Later, the apostle Paul wrote, "It is because of him that you are in Christ Jesus, who has become for us wisdom from God—that is, our righteousness, holiness and redemption" (1 Corinthians 1:30 NIV).

For those of us who believe in Jesus, He is our everything, including our righteousness. He is our Lord and Savior, our teacher and friend. . .and our satisfaction.

Jesus, thank You for satisfying my hunger and thirst for righteousness.

BLESSINGS FOR THE MERCIFUL

"God blesses those who are merciful,
for they will be shown mercy."
MATTHEW 5:7 NLT

God sent Jesus to earth so He could pour out on His Son the punishment we so richly deserve for our sins. In doing that, God the Father committed the greatest act of mercy of all time. When Jesus gave Himself up to die a horrific death on a wooden cross, He paid in full the debt none of us had any hope of paying ourselves.

In Matthew 5:7, Jesus encourages His followers to imitate His heavenly Father in showing mercy to others, saying that those who show mercy will be shown mercy in kind.

Being merciful means forgiving others who offend or hurt us. It means being compassionate to those who are still lost in sin.

If you want to receive mercy—from God and from others—then you should live a life marked by mercy. How can you be merciful to others today?

Lord Jesus, when You showered me with mercy, You did for me what I didn't deserve and could never earn. Help me to reflect You by showing mercy to others.

BLESSINGS FOR THE PURE IN HEART

"Blessed are the pure in heart, for they will see God."
MATTHEW 5:8 NIV

In Matthew 5:8, the phrase "pure in heart" refers to a heart that is blameless and clean before God, a heart that is free of the guilt of sin. Jesus promised that those who are pure in heart will one day see God, will enjoy intimacy with Him, and will inherit His eternal kingdom.

The Bible says that "the heart is deceitful above all things and beyond cure" (Jeremiah 17:9 NIV) and that "all have sinned and fall short of the glory of God" (Romans 3:23 NIV). So who are the "pure in heart" who shall "see God"?

Those who God sees as truly "pure" have been washed "in the name of the Lord Jesus Christ and by the Spirit of our God" (1 Corinthians 6:11 NIV). You are therefore declared pure and innocent through the sacrifice of Jesus, the only truly and completely pure man who ever lived.

Jesus, Psalm 51:10 (NIV) says, "Create in me a pure heart, O God." Thank You for sacrificing Yourself so God could create a clean, pure heart in me.

BLESSED PEACEMAKERS

"God blesses those who work for peace,
for they will be called the children of God."
MATTHEW 5:9 NLT

Centuries before Jesus came to earth, the prophet Isaiah wrote, "How beautiful on the mountains are the feet of those who bring good news, who proclaim peace, who bring good tidings, who proclaim salvation" (Isaiah 52:7 NIV).

In the seventh of Jesus' beatitudes, He also spoke God's blessing for those who "work for peace." Jesus wasn't talking about working for world peace or peace between people in conflict with one another (as noble and good as both may be). Rather He was talking about those who work to take Jesus' message of peace with God to the world around them.

If you are God's child, it's because you have a relationship with Him through Jesus Christ. And if you have a relationship with God through Jesus Christ, He calls you to be a "peacemaker," a man with a passion for speaking the gospel message.

Jesus, please use me as Your ambassador
for peace between God and men.

BLESSED WHEN YOU ARE PERSECUTED

"God blesses those who are persecuted for doing right, for the Kingdom of Heaven is theirs."

MATTHEW 5:10 NLT

Jesus was very clear in His teaching that living for Him wouldn't always be easy and that there would be times when we faced all sorts of opposition and persecution. After promising God's blessings for doing what is right, He went on to say, "Blessed are you when people insult you, persecute you and falsely say all kinds of evil against you because of me. Rejoice and be glad, because great is your reward in heaven, for in the same way they persecuted the prophets who were before you" (Matthew 5:11–12 NIV).

The Bible includes many examples of intense persecution of God's people. The Old Testament prophets were persecuted and so were those who preached the gospel during New Testament times. Persecution and opposition were a part of the lives of God's people in biblical times, and they will be for you today. But when it happens, you can thank God, knowing He will surely bless you.

Jesus, thank You for the blessings You bring me when I face opposition or persecution.

HIS SPIRIT IN YOU

And if the Spirit of him who raised Jesus from the dead is living in you, he who raised Christ from the dead will also give life to your mortal bodies because of his Spirit who lives in you.

Romans 8:11 NIV

As a Christian man, God has done an amazing work in you. Before you knew Jesus, you were absolutely dead in your sins and hopelessly estranged from God. But everything changed when you came to faith in Jesus. You are now spiritually alive and have been brought near—intimately near—to your adoptive heavenly Father, who sent His Holy Spirit to live within you.

The power of God Almighty raised Jesus from the dead, and He will never die again. And because we have come to Him in faith, we will also be raised from the dead—both spiritually and physically. The Holy Spirit gives spiritual life to those who trust in Jesus for their salvation, and that same Spirit will give everlasting life to our mortal bodies at the final, future resurrection.

Thank You, Jesus, that God raised You from the dead—and because You live, I too have received Your immortal life.

A MAN OF PRAYER

After leaving them, [Jesus] went up
on a mountainside to pray.
MARK 6:46 NIV

The Gospels include several accounts of Jesus praying to His Father in heaven. For example, He prayed at His baptism (Luke 3:21), before choosing His twelve disciples (Luke 6:12), before Peter's confession (Luke 9:18), at His transfiguration (Luke 9:29), and before He was arrested and crucified (John 17).

Jesus was the Son of God who had the power and authority to do everything His Father had sent Him to do. Yet, He prayed often.

Jesus was fully God and fully human. He needed to sleep, eat, and drink water—just like any of us. But to keep Himself ready to do the things He'd come to earth to do, He needed help from His Father in heaven. That means He needed to take regular time to connect with the Father through prayer.

When Jesus prayed, He set an example for each of us regarding our need for consistent, regular prayer. If Jesus, the Son of God, needed to pray, then we know we should follow His example.

Jesus, may I never neglect taking time to connect my heart to Yours through prayer.

SOMETHING FAR BETTER

But as it is, Christ has obtained a ministry that is as much more excellent than the old as the covenant he mediates is better, since it is enacted on better promises.

HEBREWS 8:6 ESV

From the time Adam and Eve's sin was revealed, God had a plan to make it possible for people to be forgiven for their sins. One day Jesus would come to earth to usher in the New Covenant, which is His promise to serve as the mediator between God and humans. In Old Testament days, the people of Israel lived under what was called the Old Covenant, which would one day be replaced by something far better.

God had intended all along to send Jesus, who would be a far better mediator of a far better covenant. God's plan for our redemption was fulfilled in Christ, who came to earth to sacrifice Himself on our behalf.

We should thank God daily that He has made a way for our new life in Jesus.

Dear Jesus, thank You for replacing the old with the new, for being my mediator who brings me close to God the Father.

A PURE CONSCIENCE

How much more will the blood of Christ,
who through the eternal Spirit offered himself
without blemish to God, purify our conscience
from dead works to serve the living God.

HEBREWS 9:14 ESV

Can you remember the last time your conscience—that inner voice that tells you that you've strayed from God in some way—wasn't clean? It never feels good when your conscience has been pricked, but it's not necessarily a bad thing when that happens, for it moves you toward confession of your sin and back toward the right road.

Sometimes, though, men find it too easy to continue punishing ourselves for the sin we lived in before we came to Christ. But here's the wonderful biblical truth about our past sins: the death of Jesus, the spotless Lamb of God, paid the price for our sins so we never have to carry the guilt of our past misdeeds.

Because of Jesus' shed blood, God chooses to forget our sins. We should do the very same thing.

Lord Jesus, thank You for removing my sins from my record permanently. Having been cleansed by You, I can serve the living God with a clean heart and conscience.

JESUS NEVER CHANGES

Jesus Christ is the same yesterday, today, and forever.

Hebrews 13:8 nlt

If there is one constant in this life, it's change. Governments change, people change—you change (you can hope your changes are for the better!). But we can always depend on Jesus to never change. Never! His character won't change, His love for you will never change, and His commitment to you will never change.

As the Father did in Old Testament times, Jesus has promised to be with you forever and always (see Matthew 28:20). He will never fail you or leave you to flounder through life on your own. He was with you yesterday, today, tomorrow. . .and through an eternity of tomorrows.

In this life you may have days when it feels like you are fighting your battles and struggles on your own. But He's always there for you, just as He promised He always would be.

Jesus never changes, so you can always depend on Him!

Jesus, thank You that You've never changed and never will change. You are my Rock, and I know I can always count on You.

ETERNAL GAINS

"If you try to hang on to your life, you will lose it. But if you give up your life for my sake and for the sake of the Good News, you will save it. And what do you benefit if you gain the whole world but lose your own soul?"

Mark 8:35–36 NLT

Many (maybe most) men in our world today are focused on the temporal: temporal wealth, temporal power, temporal happiness.

But it should not be that way for those who follow Jesus. In Mark 8:35–36, Jesus speaks a warning against making the temporal our focus. Instead, we are to avoid seeking satisfaction through worldly means and focus on following Jesus and seeking the good of His kingdom with everything we have.

So build your life and its pursuits around these words of Jesus: "Do not store up for yourselves treasures on earth. . . . But store up for yourselves treasures in heaven, where moths and vermin do not destroy, and where thieves do not break in and steal" (Matthew 6:19–20 NIV).

Lord Jesus, I give up my life to You. May my every pursuit be focused on You and Your eternal kingdom.

THE ADVOCATE

"But when the Father sends the Advocate as my representative—that is, the Holy Spirit—he will teach you everything and will remind you of everything I have told you."

JOHN 14:26 NLT

Jesus' time on earth with His beloved disciples was coming to an end. Soon Jesus would be returning to His Father in heaven, leaving the disciples behind to continue the work He had started. He had just promised He was going to ask God the Father to send them a helper—the Holy Spirit—to be with them when He was gone (see John 14:16–17).

In John 14:26, Jesus explained to the disciples that the Holy Spirit would be their teacher and would implant in their minds everything He had taught them during the past three years.

That was amazing news for the disciples two thousand years ago, and it still is today. For the same Holy Spirit who would take up residence in the disciples' hearts still lives inside each of us who trust and follow Jesus today!

Thank You, Jesus, that the Father has sent His Holy Spirit to live in my heart, teaching me the truth of the written Word, giving me strength, and guiding me in the way You want me to go.

BROUGHT NEAR TO THE GOD OF ALL COMFORT

Praise be to the God and Father of our Lord Jesus Christ, the Father of compassion and the God of all comfort, who comforts us in all our troubles, so that we can comfort those in any trouble with the comfort we ourselves receive from God.

2 Corinthians 1:3–4 niv

We are sure to go through times of trouble. We may not endure the same kind of suffering the believers in the early church endured, but modern life here on earth isn't perfect, so we're sure to go through difficulties.

The good news for those who follow Christ is that we can receive the gift of comfort from our heavenly Father—sometimes through the ministry of others, sometimes through the Holy Spirit's comforting work, and (most often) through Jesus, the ultimate source of comfort (see 2 Corinthians 1:5).

Jesus, You comfort me during difficult times—sometimes through a trusted Christian friend but always through time spent with You through Your written Word. Thank You!

A NO-LOSE SITUATION

For to me to live is Christ, and to die is gain.

PHILIPPIANS 1:21 ESV

The apostle Paul wrote his letter to the Philippian church while suffering in prison, and he knew it was possible that he could be martyred for Christ. Yet, his response to the situation wasn't one of fear of death.

In Philippians 1:21, Paul essentially says, "If I live longer, I get to continue serving Jesus. But if I die, I get to go be with Jesus and see Him face-to-face. Either way I can't lose!"

God has given each of us a certain number of days to live. Like Paul, we should thank Him for every day we can serve Him. But we can also thank God for the assurance that should death come soon, we'll get to be in Jesus' wonderful presence that much sooner.

Lord Jesus, because I belong to You, living a long life means I get to serve and glorify You here on earth even longer. But if I should pass on today, all the better—because then I get to be in Your presence.

OUR CITIZENSHIP

Our citizenship is in heaven, from which we also eagerly wait for a Savior, the Lord Jesus Christ.

Philippians 3:20 HCSB

Being a United States citizen means something to us Americans. We have many rights and privileges conferred on us—too many to list here. But as Christian men, we now live in a "home away from home" here on earth. As Philippians 3:20 says, "Our citizenship is in heaven."

We can and should do all we can to influence individuals, our culture, and our government toward God and godly principles. But we must do those things realizing that this world is not our ultimate home, that because we know and follow Jesus, we have eternal homes in God's kingdom.

Believers have so much to look forward to beyond this life. Let us all live our lives here with an eye that looks beyond the here and now.

Lord Jesus, as a living American man, I have my citizenship here in the United States. But more than that, I am a citizen of Your eternal kingdom in heaven.

WHEN YOU GIVE

"When you give to the needy, sound no trumpet before you, as the hypocrites do in the synagogues and in the streets. . . . But when you give to the needy, do not let your left hand know what your right hand is doing, so that your giving may be in secret. And your Father who sees in secret will reward you."

MATTHEW 6:2–4 ESV

In Jesus' day, the rich and powerful often went out of their way to make sure others knew about their giving so they could be seen as generous. But Jesus called His followers to something different, teaching them that when they gave to the needy, they should do it in secret so God would reward them for their hearts of true generosity.

The Bible says that God loves and blesses those who give willingly and cheerfully (see 2 Corinthians 9:6–7). So give! But do it privately and without seeking human recognition.

Jesus, help me to be a generous person who doesn't need human recognition when I give.

HE LIVES IN YOU!

For God wanted them to know that the riches and glory of Christ are for you Gentiles, too. And this is the secret: Christ lives in you. This gives you assurance of sharing his glory.

Colossians 1:27 NLT

Today's scripture verse shares with us a secret—a wonderful, life-changing secret. Even though Jesus has returned to heaven where He sits at the right hand of God, He is still with us, living in and through us.

Before Jesus returned to heaven, He instructed His followers to take His gospel message to the world around them—and then He promised them, "Surely I am with you always, to the very end of the age" (Matthew 28:20 NIV). That promise is for us today too. And knowing that Jesus is with us—living in us—we can go through each day with the absolute assurance that we can handle anything the world throws our way.

Lord Jesus, thank You that You actually live in me—encouraging me, strengthening me, guiding me. . .and loving me.

"FOLLOW ME"

"If anyone serves Me, he must follow Me. Where I am, there My servant also will be. If anyone serves Me, the Father will honor him."

John 12:26 HCSB

As Jesus began His earthly ministry, He called twelve men to be His disciples. He called the first two—Peter and Andrew—with the words "Come, follow me" (Matthew 4:19 NIV). This call wasn't just to follow when the disciples felt like it or to follow at a distance (like so many did). The word *follow* meant that these men were going to accompany Jesus everywhere He went, learning from Him, fellowshipping with Him, learning to trust and obey Him, and living by His example.

That's what it means to be a disciple of Christ—and it's what He desires for every Christian even today. Jesus wants all who believe in Him to follow in a way that enables and empowers them to serve Him and follow Him with everything they have.

Lord Jesus, I want to be Your disciple, and that means I need to follow You with my whole heart.

A NEW CREATION

Therefore, if anyone is in Christ, the new creation has come: The old has gone, the new is here!
2 Corinthians 5:17 niv

God did an amazing miracle when you came to faith in Jesus. He took a helpless, lost, sin-filled creature and gave you a new life, a new identity, a new way of thinking, and a new purpose. You may look like the same person, and your personality may mostly be the same; but the way you think, live, and relate to Him and others has not just been changed but has been transformed. That's because Jesus lives inside you in the person of the Holy Spirit, which changes everything.

But it doesn't end there. God makes you more and more like Jesus every day. Your old way of thinking and living is replaced by something much better: the abundant life Jesus promised you!

Dear Jesus, thank You for making me a new creation. Thank You for replacing the sinful, dark side of me with Your goodness. You've done what I could never do for myself.

A MODEL PRAYER: "OUR FATHER IN HEAVEN"

" 'Our Father in heaven.' "

MATTHEW 6:9 NIV

Jesus taught His followers the most important aspects of prayer when He shared what we now call "The Lord's Prayer" (Matthew 6:9–13). He began His model for prayer by instructing us to address God as "Our Father in heaven."

In Jesus' day Jewish people didn't call God "Father." But Jesus did, and He said we should do the same. He wanted His followers to understand that God was not just our Creator and Redeemer, not just a holy, all-powerful Lord of all, but also our loving heavenly Father.

Paul later wrote of the Father/child relationship: "The Spirit you received brought about your adoption to sonship. And by him we cry, 'Abba, Father'" (Romans 8:15 NIV).

When you pray, remember that in Christ you are God's beloved child and He is your Father in heaven who has given you the privilege of calling Him "Abba, Father."

Thank You, Jesus, for adopting me into God's family and for giving me the privilege of addressing God as "Father."

A MODEL PRAYER: "HALLOWED BE YOUR NAME"

" 'Hallowed be your name.' "

MATTHEW 6:9 NIV

We don't often hear the word *hallowed* spoken these days. It's a slightly outdated term, but one with deep, important meaning when it comes to how we should address God in prayer. It means to make holy or to honor as sacred.

When Jesus instructed His followers—including us today—to pray, "Hallowed be your name," He was teaching that we should always honor God's name, as He is worthy, and never take that name lightly or flippantly.

In the Old Testament, God was called "the Most High God," "Jehovah," "El Shaddai," "Adonai," and other names that honored Him as the great I AM.

God is your loving heavenly Father, and you can address Him that way. But always remember when you pray to Him that His name should always be hallowed.

Lord Jesus, thank You for reminding me that while God is my loving heavenly Father, He is still the Most High God—and I must always honor Him and His name appropriately.

A MODEL PRAYER: "YOUR KINGDOM COME"

" 'Your kingdom come, your will be done, on earth as it is in heaven.' "

MATTHEW 6:10 NIV

Left on our own, humans have a great capacity for selfishness and self-interest, and that's why Jesus instructed us to pray according to God's will—both here and in heaven. Effective, God-honoring prayer makes His glory and agenda the top priority.

Jesus set our example for this kind of prayer on the night He was arrested. He knew the pain and suffering He was about to endure, and He wondered if there was another way to rescue humankind from the consequences of sin. But Jesus was submitted to His Father's will and plan, so He prayed, "Yet not my will, but yours be done" (Luke 22:42 NIV).

When you pray, you will do well to place your own will and desires far behind God's glory and what He wants.

Thank You, Jesus, for not just telling me to pray according to God's will and glory but also for setting a perfect example when You prayed, "Not my will, but yours be done."

A MODEL PRAYER: "GIVE US TODAY OUR DAILY BREAD"

" *'Give us today our daily bread.'* "
MATTHEW 6:11 NIV

In ages past, some believed that when Jesus spoke the words in Matthew 6:11, He was using the word *bread* metaphorically. What He meant, they believed, was that believers should ask God to provide for our spiritual needs. Certainly, He couldn't have been talking about something so temporal, so "secular," as food and other provisions.

But when Jesus instructed us to pray, "Give us today our daily bread," He really was instructing us to ask God to meet our daily temporal needs, such as food, water, shelter, and anything else we truly need.

God cares about your spiritual needs, and He has done everything necessary to provide for them. But He also cares about everyday physical needs, and Jesus encourages you to pray and ask God to meet yours.

Jesus, thank You for God's willingness to meet my family's temporal needs—such as food, water, and shelter—when I simply tell You what I need.

A MODEL PRAYER: "FORGIVE US OUR DEBTS"

" 'And forgive us our debts, as we also have forgiven our debtors.' "
MATTHEW 6:12 NIV

Jesus came to earth to provide forgiveness of sin and to make a way for imperfect humans to inherit God's perfect eternal kingdom. In Matthew 6:12, Jesus equates sin with indebtedness to a holy-but-forgiving God.

Humans share many things in common, and one of them is a debt to God so deep that we have no hope of repaying it. But Jesus took that debt on Himself and nullified it for good.

When we pray, "Forgive us our debts," we can do so in the confidence that God will hear us and do what we've asked. As the apostle John wrote, "If we confess our sins, he is faithful and just and will forgive us our sins and purify us from all unrighteousness" (1 John 1:9 NIV).

Lord Jesus, in my sins I have a debt I have no hope of repaying. Thank You for taking that debt from me and declaring it "paid in full." Thank You, also, for forgiving and purifying me when I confess my sins to You.

A MODEL PRAYER: "LEAD US NOT INTO TEMPTATION"

" 'And lead us not into temptation,
but deliver us from the evil one.' "
MATTHEW 6:13 NIV

The apostle James wrote, "God cannot be tempted by evil, nor does he tempt anyone; but each person is tempted when they are dragged away by their own evil desire and enticed" (James 1:13–14 NIV).

At a glance Jesus' words in Matthew 6:13 seem to imply that God might lead us into the temptation to sin. But it is actually a plea for God to protect us, to guide us away from situations where temptation lurks. It is a prayer for the wisdom we need to avoid people and circumstances that could possibly cause us to stray.

God has promised to keep us from temptation that is too strong for us to handle (see 1 Corinthians 10:13). When we access that promise in prayer, we need to do our part to avoid temptation before it can overtake us.

Lord Jesus, temptation will always be a part of my life here on earth. Please give me wisdom to avoid temptation and the strength to overcome it.

A COMMANDMENT TO LOVE

"'Love the Lord your God with all your heart and with all your soul and with all your mind and with all your strength.' The second is this: 'Love your neighbor as yourself.' There is no commandment greater than these."

MARK 12:30–31 NIV

One day a Jewish religious teacher asked Jesus which Old Testament law was most important. Jesus answered by quoting Deuteronomy 6:5 (NIV), which says, "Love the LORD your God with all your heart and with all your soul and with all your strength," and Leviticus 19:18 (NIV), which tells us to "love your neighbor as yourself."

Love God and love your neighbors. It really is that simple!

On a practical level, loving your neighbor as yourself means treating people with kindness, patience, and hospitality, showing respect and civility to those with whom you disagree, and making a life goal to help meet other people's needs.

Loving Jesus and your neighbor from your heart helps others, and it puts you in position to receive His blessings.

Jesus, I want others to see You in me. Help me to love from my heart and in my actions.

THE KEY TO EFFECTIVE PRAYER

"But if you remain in me and my words remain in you, you may ask for anything you want, and it will be granted!"

John 15:7 NLT

In John 15:7, Jesus made a powerful promise to His disciples, telling them that if they remained in Him and His words, they could expect to receive anything they asked for in prayer.

That promise was for His disciples when He was still on earth, and it's for faithful disciples today as well.

Remaining in Jesus means clinging faithfully to Him each day, allowing His words to penetrate and remain in our hearts, accepting His authority, and remaining in constant contact with Him through prayer.

When we find that our prayers seem to go unanswered or are not as effective as they should be, it may be time to evaluate ourselves to see if we're lagging in our relationship with Jesus. When we remain in Him, we can enjoy a powerful prayer life that brings results.

Lord Jesus, may I remain in You every day and in every way so I may receive what I ask for in prayer.

CALLED TO SERVE IN HUMILITY

"And since I, your Lord and Teacher, have washed your feet, you ought to wash each other's feet."
JOHN 13:14 NLT

After Jesus had completed the humble, highly symbolic act of washing His disciples' feet, He let them know they were to follow His example.

When Jesus commanded His disciples to "wash each other's feet," He was calling them to live lives of humble, loving, sacrificial service to one another—the same kind of loving service He had demonstrated during the entirety of His earthly ministry. It's the kind of love in action Paul wrote about in Romans 12:10–13 (NIV): "Be devoted to one another in love. Honor one another above yourselves. Never be lacking in zeal, but keep your spiritual fervor, serving the Lord. Be joyful in hope, patient in affliction, faithful in prayer. Share with the Lord's people who are in need."

You can be sure that there are Christian brothers and sisters in your life who could benefit from a humble act of service. How can you "wash someone's feet" today?

***Lord, help me to be a humble servant—
to You and to those who are Yours.***

FORWARD FOCUS

Brothers, I do not consider myself to have taken hold of it. But one thing I do: Forgetting what is behind and reaching forward to what is ahead, I pursue as my goal the prize promised by God's heavenly call in Christ Jesus.

Philippians 3:13–14 HCSB

There's nothing wrong with fondly remembering the things God has done in and through us since the day we came to faith in Jesus Christ. In fact, God can use the past to teach us important lessons and to give us reasons to praise and thank Him for His goodness. We shouldn't try to completely forget the past, but we also shouldn't let the past keep us from looking forward to what God has in store for us today and in the future.

God has big plans for you—as a Christian man, a mentor and a church member. He wants you to grow spiritually—and the future is where your growth takes place. So remember all God has done for you in Christ Jesus, but keep looking forward as you take your journey of faith in Jesus.

Lord Jesus, keep my eyes focused on what You have in store for me—today and in the future.

OVERCOMING THE EVIL ONE

I am writing to you, fathers, because you know him who is from the beginning. I am writing to you, young men, because you have overcome the evil one.

1 John 2:13 NIV

Ephesians 6:12 (NIV) tells believers that "our struggle is not against flesh and blood, but against the rulers, against the authorities, against the powers of this dark world and against the spiritual forces of evil in the heavenly realms."

This is a good definition of what is called "spiritual warfare"—a war the apostle John said we can win when we grow in our walk with Jesus and keep ourselves in God's Word. Our ultimate spiritual enemy, the devil, has already lost the biggest battle with those of us who trust Jesus as our Lord and Savior. Now his goal is to keep us from living a victorious life of faith and obedience.

But when we cling to Jesus and walk in God's Word, we can live in the fulfilled promise of overcoming the evil one.

Lord Jesus, may I always cling to You and Your truth so I can overcome the devil and his spiritual cohorts.

ABIDING IN CHRIST'S LOVE

"If you keep my commandments, you will abide in my love, just as I have kept my Father's commandments and abide in his love."

JOHN 15:10 ESV

Jesus set an example of full obedience to God in every way. He spoke the words His Father wanted Him to speak, did the things He wanted Him to do, and loved the way He wanted Him to love. When His time of teaching and miracle-working on this earth was finished, He obeyed God by willingly giving Himself up to die for our sins.

Jesus remained in His Father's love by keeping His commandments. And in John 15:10, He called His disciples to remain in His love through their obedience to their Master. This tells us that the mark of a true disciple of Christ is keeping His commandments.

Unbelief always leads to disobedience, but abiding in Christ's love means obeying Him, and obeying Him means hearing and believing His every promise and every command.

Lord Jesus, I want to abide in Your love every day. Help me to live a life of faith and obedience so I can remain in Your love.

"FORGIVE THEM"

Jesus said, "Father, forgive them, for they do not know what they are doing." And they divided up his clothes by casting lots.

LUKE 23:34 NIV

The four Gospels record seven statements from the mouth of Jesus—the sinless, perfect Lamb of God who had broken no laws, either of man or the Almighty—as He hung dying from a Roman cross. The most amazing of those statements, recorded in Luke 23:34, is His plea to the Father to forgive His tormentors.

Historians have described crucifixion as one of the cruelest, most humiliating methods of execution of all time. Yet Jesus never protested, never expressed anger, and never asked God to rescue Him. Instead He forgave.

Jesus suffered in ways we can't even imagine so we could be forgiven for our sins. And even when He was a few hours from death, He set history's perfect example of what a heart of forgiveness looks like.

Jesus, even as You hung from a cross in agony, You chose to forgive. Thank You for being the perfect example of forgiveness.

UNWAVERING CONFIDENCE

And he said to them, "Why are you afraid,
O you of little faith?" Then he rose and rebuked the
winds and the sea, and there was a great calm.
Matthew 8:26 esv

Jesus' disciples were faced with a test of their faith as wind-driven waves crashed over the sides of their boat. They failed that test—badly. They were in a state of panic, even though Jesus was with them. . .sleeping.

"Lord, save us! We're going to drown!" they screamed (Matthew 8:25 niv). Jesus awoke from His nap, but instead of dealing with the problem at hand right away, He first scolded them for their unbelief.

"O you of little faith"! The disciples must have felt the pain of embarrassment as they heard those words from their Master.

Jesus wants His followers to have unwavering confidence in Him at all times. Even when we feel as though the storms of life are about to take us down for good. Even when it feels like He is silent. That's what real faith looks like.

Jesus, teach me to have unwavering confidence in You, especially when I'm afraid, worried, or stressed.

LIGHT OVERCOMES DARKNESS

Life was in Him, and that life was the light of men. That light shines in the darkness, yet the darkness did not overcome it.

John 1:4–5 HCSB

How would you describe the word *darkness*? First of all, darkness is the lack of light. When you are in a place of absolute physical darkness, you can't see anything, no matter how long you allow for your eyes to adjust. There is only inky blackness. . .unless someone shines a light into that place.

The Bible teaches that our world is in a perpetual state of spiritual darkness. People who are living in this world are spiritually dead, even though they live, breathe, and move. But Jesus came into the world to overcome the darkness by shining God's light. That is why He said, "I am the light of the world. Whoever follows me will never walk in darkness, but will have the light of life" (John 8:12 NIV).

John 1:4–5 says this world's darkness will never overcome the light of Jesus. He came to bring light and life to those who choose to follow Him.

Thank You, Jesus, for defeating darkness and for being my life and my light.

REVEALING GOD

And we know that the Son of God has come and has given us understanding, so that we may know him who is true; and we are in him who is true, in his Son Jesus Christ. He is the true God and eternal life.

1 John 5:20 ESV

The apostle John wrote 1 John 5:20 several decades after traveling with Jesus, watching Jesus, and hearing Jesus' amazing teaching. John knew better than anyone that Jesus had come to earth to reveal God to the whole world.

Knowing Jesus means knowing our heavenly Father. Through Jesus, God has given us understanding of who He is and what He is really like. Not only that, He has given us the ability to know Him personally—not just theoretically or academically, but *personally.*

Jesus, God's only Son, came to earth to die for the sins of humankind. But He also revealed God and His true nature to us through His teaching and through the examples He set—of righteous living and of love in action.

Jesus, thank You for coming to earth to reveal the Father and show us what He is really like.

GROWING IN JESUS

But you, beloved, building yourselves up in your most holy faith and praying in the Holy Spirit, keep yourselves in the love of God, waiting for the mercy of our Lord Jesus Christ that leads to eternal life.

JUDE 20–21 ESV

The epistle of Jude includes fierce condemnations of people we might think of as "false converts" within the church. But in the above verses, Jude encourages true believers to take responsibility for their own spiritual growth.

Jesus has already done everything needed to bring us into eternal fellowship with God. But that doesn't mean we shouldn't do the things necessary to build ourselves up in our "most holy faith." That means spending time every day fellowshipping with God through reading His written Word and "praying in the Holy Spirit." When we do those simple things, we keep our relationship with Jesus fresh and growing.

Any good relationship takes work and commitment. That includes your relationship with God through Jesus Christ.

Lord Jesus, I want my relationship with You to grow deeper and stronger every day. Thank You for giving me Your Word and the privilege of talking to You through prayer.

ACCEPTING ONE ANOTHER

Accept one another, then, just as Christ accepted you, in order to bring praise to God.
ROMANS 15:7 NIV

Think about the day you came to Jesus for salvation. On that day Jesus accepted you—a man hopelessly lost in sin and rebellion—into His eternal family. There was nothing about you that made you acceptable to a holy God, yet He extended His grace and mercy—simply because you believed.

Romans 15:6 (NIV) says that "with one mind and one voice you may glorify the God and Father of our Lord Jesus Christ." Then Paul goes on in verse 7 to encourage believers to "accept one another. . .just as Christ accepted you."

Jesus wants unity within His body, the church, and that happens when we set aside our differences and focus on the one who has brought us together.

Lord Jesus, may I never allow petty differences between me and other believers to divide us. Instead, I will strive to accept others as You have accepted me.

WHEN YOU FEEL HATED

"If the world hates you, keep in mind that it hated me first. If you belonged to the world, it would love you as its own. As it is, you do not belong to the world, but I have chosen you out of the world. That is why the world hates you."

John 15:18–19 NIV

Have you ever been in a social situation where you felt like you didn't fit in—or worse yet, felt rejected or disliked? As a Christian man living in a sin-darkened world, there *will* be times when you feel that way.

Those who follow Jesus stand for things the world hates. Jesus warned His disciples that it would be that way, and it's still that way today. But we should never allow the difficulties we face because we profess faith in Jesus to discourage us or cause us to shrink back in fear or discouragement.

Always remember: you don't belong to this world; you belong to Jesus!

Lord Jesus, I don't enjoy being ridiculed or rejected, but I am committed to following You no matter what. Give me the courage to stand for and live for You, no matter what it costs me.

HE DWELT AMONG US

And the Word was made flesh, and dwelt among us, (and we beheld his glory, the glory as of the only begotten of the Father,) full of grace and truth.

John 1:14 KJV

John 1:14 tells us that the eternal living Word—Jesus, the one and only Son of God, the one filled with His Father's grace and truth—*chose* to come to earth to live as a man and dwell among sinful, lost humanity.

Think for a minute about what Jesus gave up just to come to earth to be with us, to teach us, and to die for us. He humbled Himself and left His perfect, eternal home in heaven where He enjoyed uninterrupted intimate fellowship with His Father to spend more than three decades in this dark, fallen world where He lived life among the neediest among us.

And He did that because He *wanted* to. What a Savior He is!

Jesus, thank You for coming to earth to teach, lead, and save people like me. May I never forget what You gave up just to come here.

REWARDS FOR CONQUERING

The one who conquers, I will grant him to sit with me on my throne, as I also conquered and sat down with my Father on his throne.

REVELATION 3:21 ESV

In Revelation 3:14–21, Jesus chides the lukewarm Laodicean church, which had fallen into apathy and complacency in its relationship with the Lord, but He also makes the church members an amazing promise, one that applies to us today.

Jesus promised the Laodiceans an eternal blessing—that they could "sit with me on my throne"—if they would simply begin again to deny themselves and follow Him faithfully and wholeheartedly.

Like the Laodiceans, we can easily find ourselves becoming lukewarm because of worldly concerns and distractions. But Jesus calls the lukewarm Christian to put Him back at the center of his heart and life. When we answer that call, we put ourselves in position to receive amazing eternal blessings.

Lord Jesus, it's too easy to fall into a life of lukewarm faith. I don't want that to happen to me. Instead, I want to take up my cross daily, deny myself, and follow You with my whole heart.

MADE ALIVE IN CHRIST

For since death came through a man, the resurrection of the dead comes also through a man. For as in Adam all die, so in Christ all will be made alive.

1 Corinthians 15:21–22 niv

When the devil tempted Adam and Eve into sinning against God, it stained humankind and all creation with sin and death. But from the very beginning God had a plan to defeat Satan and his diabolical works. That is what He meant when He told the serpent, "And I will put enmity between you and the woman, and between your offspring and hers; he will crush your head, and you will strike his heel" (Genesis 3:15 niv).

The consequences of sin, namely physical and spiritual death, have fallen on all men, but Jesus brought each of us who believe in Him eternal hope and life. That hope is what 1 Corinthians 15:21–22 calls "the resurrection of the dead"—and it's the promise of a new body that will live forever in heaven.

Jesus, thank You for defeating the devil and his evil works so I can live forever in a resurrected body.

GOD'S GIFT TO THE CHURCH

Therefore, since He has been exalted to the right hand of God and has received from the Father the promised Holy Spirit, He has poured out what you both see and hear.

ACTS 2:33 HCSB

The day of Pentecost (see Acts 2) marked the beginning of great things for the fledgling church. On that day God fulfilled Jesus' promise to send the Holy Spirit to teach, guide, and empower the Christians who were gathered in Jerusalem. God's Spirit had come, and things would change in a profound way.

The most amazing example of change was in Peter—the disciple of Jesus who often said and did the wrong things and who had denied even knowing Jesus after His arrest. This same Peter, now filled with the Holy Spirit, preached an amazing evangelistic sermon, leading three thousand people to repent of their sins and turn to Jesus for their salvation.

Two millennia later, that same Holy Spirit lives in and empowers you!

Jesus, thank You for Your fulfilled promise of the Holy Spirit. With Him empowering me, I can be the man You've created me to be and do the things You've called me to do.

POWER IN WEAKNESS

But he said to me, "My grace is sufficient for you, for my power is made perfect in weakness." Therefore I will boast all the more gladly about my weaknesses, so that Christ's power may rest on me.

2 Corinthians 12:9 NIV

In 2 Corinthians 12:7 (NIV) the apostle Paul makes mention of a "thorn in [his] flesh." Three times Paul asked God to remove this mysterious issue from him, but he found no relief. Instead, God told him, "My grace is sufficient for you, for my power is made perfect in weakness."

Paul probably still wanted relief, but he wanted to glorify Jesus even more. God's answer wasn't what Paul had hoped for, but he listened to God and found divine purpose in what he had been enduring. Instead of complaining or feeling sorry for himself, Paul humbled himself so that the power of Christ could be more fully demonstrated in him.

Whether or not God removes our personal "thorns," His grace is always more than enough for us.

Dear Jesus, when I suffer from my personal "thorns," You care. And even if You choose to leave them in my life, Your grace gives me the strength to endure and glorify You.

REAL FAITH

For in Christ Jesus neither circumcision nor uncircumcision has any value. The only thing that counts is faith expressing itself through love.

GALATIANS 5:6 NIV

In Galatians 5:6 Paul goes out of his way to counter false teaching of Judaizers, who told the Christians in Galatia that they must be circumcised in order to be made right with God. He essentially told them that in Jesus it didn't matter whether they were circumcised and that they must not put their trust in Levitical law.

But Paul didn't stop at what the Galatians shouldn't do; he went on to tell them that the only thing that mattered was a faith in Jesus Christ that expresses itself through love for others.

Paul also wrote that "whoever loves others has fulfilled the law" (Romans 13:8 NIV). These two verses taken together show us that real saving faith in Jesus is always proven through attitudes and acts of love.

Lord Jesus, You want me to have faith in You. Help me to demonstrate that faith in how I love others.

KNOWING GOD

"Now this is eternal life: that they know you, the only true God, and Jesus Christ, whom you have sent."

JOHN 17:3 NIV

On the night Jesus was arrested, He showed His heart for His ultimate mission when He prayed the prayer in John 17:3. Jesus and His Father in heaven were of one heart and mind in their passionate desire that men could personally know God through the one He had sent to earth to rescue sinners.

Eternal life is God's free gift, received at the very moment we trusted Jesus as our Savior. Eternal life is also knowing God on a personal level and being welcomed into His forever family.

No man can know the Father apart from the Son. But when you know and trust Jesus as your Lord and Savior, you can know God not just as your Creator but also as your own loving heavenly Father.

Jesus, because I know You, I know the Father. Help me to always communicate that without You no one can know Your Father in heaven.

CREATED ANEW FOR GOOD THINGS

For we are God's masterpiece. He has created us anew in Christ Jesus, so we can do the good things he planned for us long ago.

EPHESIANS 2:10 NLT

The Bible teaches that the Christian is saved only as a result of God's amazing grace. Our salvation has nothing to do with our own good works and everything to do with God's graciousness toward us (see Ephesians 2:8–9). That is how God makes us His own "masterpiece."

But God didn't "[create] us anew in Christ Jesus" so we can just wait around to enter God's eternal, heavenly kingdom. As God's masterpieces, we are called to glorify the Lord by doing good things, things He had planned for us long before we were born.

When God first saved you, He gave you His Holy Spirit—and He gives you the ability and the desire to give, love, and serve.

Jesus, thank You for making me Your own masterpiece. Show me the good works You have planned for me so I can bring glory to Your wonderful name.

OUR SUFFERING SAVIOR

But he was pierced for our transgressions, he was crushed for our iniquities; the punishment that brought us peace was on him, and by his wounds we are healed.

Isaiah 53:5 niv

Isaiah 53 is about what many call the "Suffering Servant" because it describes in great detail what the Messiah would endure for His people. Isaiah wrote, "He was despised and rejected by mankind, a man of suffering, and familiar with pain. . . . Surely he took up our pain and bore our suffering, yet we considered him punished by God, stricken by him, and afflicted" (Isaiah 53:3–4 niv).

Isaiah follows these words with the reason *why* Jesus would one day suffer so terribly. The Messiah, Isaiah wrote, was "pierced for our transgressions" and "crushed for our iniquities."

Jesus didn't just suffer; He suffered *in our place.* As sinners, we were hopelessly separated from God and due the punishment for our wrongdoing. But Jesus willingly took the punishment in our place so we could be eternally reconciled with God.

Lord Jesus, thank You for voluntarily suffering so I could be forgiven for my sins.

BECAUSE WE'VE WANDERED. . .

We all, like sheep, have gone astray, each of us has turned to our own way; and the Lord has laid on him the iniquity of us all.

Isaiah 53:6 niv

Most people in ancient Israel were familiar with sheep, and they knew that they are, in more modern terms, dim bulbs of the animal kingdom. Without a shepherd to watch over them, sheep are as likely as not to wander away from the flock, where they could be easy pickings for hungry predators.

The Old Testament prophet Isaiah, writing under the inspiration of the Holy Spirit, likened rebellious humanity to sheep that had wandered off into dangerous territory—places where our spiritual enemy can easily devour us.

But Isaiah also wrote that God had a plan to bring us back to Himself, where we can be safe and secure under our Shepherd-Father's watchful eye. That plan was to send His Son, Jesus Christ, into the world and to lay on Him all our sin at a place called Calvary.

Thank You, Jesus, for taking upon Yourself the consequences of sin for a wandering sheep like me.

GOD REVEALED

No one has ever seen God. But the unique One, who is himself God, is near to the Father's heart. He has revealed God to us.

JOHN 1:18 NLT

The Old Testament includes many examples of men hearing God, speaking with God, and catching glimpses of God's essence. But no one—not even great men of God like Moses, Elijah, or Isaiah—actually saw God face-to-face. Today, we see God's glory in a limited way, in the physical world and through the amazing things He has done, but none of us has seen God in all His glory.

In the above scripture verse, John wrote that Jesus revealed God to us when He came to earth to live as one who is 100 percent God and 100 percent human.

Jesus truly is one of a kind, God in the flesh, and through Him we can know the invisible God in a very real, very personal way.

Lord Jesus, thank You for revealing the heavenly Father to me. Please reveal more and more of Him to me every day.

SENT BY JESUS

Again Jesus said, "Peace be with you! As the Father has sent me, I am sending you." And with that he breathed on them and said, "Receive the Holy Spirit."

JOHN 20:21–22 NIV

From the very moment Jesus called His disciples to come and follow Him, He had a world-changing mission for them. And after they had spent three years following Him, listening to His teaching, witnessing His miracles, and seeing Him die and then live again, it was time for them to follow their calling.

"As the Father has sent me, I am sending you," He told them, echoing His pre-crucifixion prayer. "As you sent me into the world, I have sent them into the world" (John 17:18 NIV).

The disciples' marching orders were simple: to continue Jesus' work after He returned to His Father in heaven. Our mission today as Christ's disciples is the same. Each of us is to be His ambassador to this world.

Jesus, God sent You to earth to live among sinful people and to rescue us from the horrible grip of sin. May I be faithful to Your calling to take the gospel to the world around me.

THAT YOU MAY KNOW

I write these things to you who believe in the name of the Son of God, that you may know that you have eternal life.

1 John 5:13 ESV

"That you may know. . ." John's focus in his first epistle was to give those who believe in Jesus, the Son of God, assurance (or as the old hymn calls it, "blessed assurance") that their sins were forgiven and that they could look forward to a glorious eternity in God's eternal kingdom.

We, as believers, must never allow our moments of doubt to cause us to forget that the blood of Jesus has saved us from the terrible penalty we deserve because of our sin. Jesus died for us and was raised from the dead three days later. And because He lives, the power of sin and death are broken (see 1 Corinthians 15:54–57).

Thank You, Jesus, that I don't have to wonder if I have eternal life or hope I have eternal life. Because You shed Your blood for me, I can know I will spend eternity with You in heaven.

BE READY ALWAYS

And, behold, I come quickly; and my reward is with me, to give every man according as his work shall be.

REVELATION 22:12 KJV

Late in His earthly ministry Jesus told His disciples, "So you also must be ready, because the Son of Man will come at an hour when you do not expect him" (Matthew 24:44 NIV). He also told them, "But about that day or hour no one knows, not even the angels in heaven, nor the Son, but only the Father" (Matthew 24:36 NIV).

In today's scripture verse, Jesus promises to return "quickly," bringing with Him rewards for every man according to what he has done during his life on earth. This should encourage each of us who follows Jesus to always be ready and to work to "store up for yourselves treasures in heaven, where moths and vermin do not destroy, and where thieves do not break in and steal" (Matthew 6:20 NIV).

Jesus, I look forward to the day You return. May I remain faithful to You so I can receive the eternal rewards You've promised.

THE PRECIOUS BLOOD OF JESUS

Knowing that you were ransomed from the futile ways inherited from your forefathers, not with perishable things such as silver or gold, but with the precious blood of Christ, like that of a lamb without blemish or spot.

1 Peter 1:18–19 ESV

Jesus spoke of the value of humans to God when He said, "Are not two sparrows sold for a penny? Yet not one of them will fall to the ground outside your Father's care. And even the very hairs of your head are all numbered. So don't be afraid; you are worth more than many sparrows" (Matthew 10:29–31 NIV).

Humanity was the crown jewel of God's creation, the only created thing made in His image. And we are of such value to Him that He gave the very best He had to save us from eternal destruction—His own Son who shed His precious blood (worth far more than any amount of gold or silver) to pay for our sins.

Today think about this: *Jesus shed His precious blood. . .for me!*

Lord Jesus, thank You for shedding Your precious blood, which is of infinitely greater value than even the most valuable metals or stones.

LOOK UP TO JESUS

"Just as Moses lifted up the snake in the wilderness, so the Son of Man must be lifted up, that everyone who believes may have eternal life in him."

JOHN 3:14–15 NIV

Numbers 21 tells the story of how God sent highly venomous snakes as punishment for the Israelites' complaining and unbelief. Moses prayed for the people, and God commanded him to fashion a bronze serpent and place it atop a long pole so the people could look at it and live.

The Israelites could not be saved by killing off the snakes. Only provision by God Himself gave them any hope of escaping death. The same is true for sinful man even today.

You were not—and could not be—saved from the consequences of your sin through any self-effort, any good works, or any vows to stop sinning. You were saved by looking to God's perfect sin sacrifice: Jesus, who was lifted up on the cross to die so those who looked to Him in faith could live eternally.

Jesus, thank You for allowing Yourself to be lifted up on the cross so people can look up to You and be saved from the consequences of their sin.

WORSHIPPING GOD THROUGH SERVING OTHERS

And he answered, "If you had a sheep that fell into a well on the Sabbath, wouldn't you work to pull it out? Of course you would. And how much more valuable is a person than a sheep! Yes, the law permits a person to do good on the Sabbath."

MATTHEW 12:11–12 NLT

Jesus used His healing of a man with a withered hand on a Sabbath day to teach that acts of compassion are not just permissible but blessed on the day of rest. While the self-righteous, legalistic Jewish religious leaders saw what Jesus had done as an unlawful act of work on the Sabbath, Jesus saw it as an opportunity to do good for someone in need.

Today we, as Christians, consider Sunday our day of worship. But we shouldn't think of worship as just the act of going to church and singing songs to God. We can worship and honor God by blessing those in need. For today's Christ follower, every day is a good one to worship God through service to others.

Jesus, You have shown me that any day is a good day to bless others in Your name.

COMMITTED TO THE FATHER'S WILL

Going a little farther, he fell with his face to the ground and prayed, "My Father, if it is possible, may this cup be taken from me. Yet not as I will, but as you will."

Matthew 26:39 niv

During Jesus' time on earth, He was not only 100 percent divine but also 100 percent human. In today's scripture verse, which is part of Matthew's account of Jesus' heart-wrenching prayer in the garden of Gethsemane, Jesus asked His heavenly Father if there was any other way to bring salvation and forgiveness to lost and sinful humans.

Jesus was painfully honest with the Father as He humbly stated His own desires. Yet, He also said He was 100 percent committed to doing the Father's will and not His own.

That terrible night in the garden, Jesus set for us an example of prayer—honest prayer, humble prayer. . .and prayer that is fully submitted to the will of our Father in heaven.

Jesus, may I always remember to submit myself to the Father's perfect will, even when that will takes me to places I'd rather not go.

"WHOEVER COMES TO ME. . ."

"All those the Father gives me will come to me, and whoever comes to me I will never drive away."
JOHN 6:37 NIV

People are capable of voicing all sorts of reasons why they can't or won't come to Jesus for salvation. Probably the saddest of all excuses is that they've sinned so terribly and for so long that there is no way a holy, righteous God would ever allow them into His eternal kingdom.

In today's scripture verse, Jesus spoke a short message for people who believe He will accept them. That message is simply that everyone who comes to Him, trusting Him for salvation, will most certainly be accepted into God's eternal family. Salvation is available to all who come to Christ—and that includes the very worst of sinners.

When you meet someone who believes he has sinned too much and rebelled against God for too long to ever be saved, remember Jesus' beautiful promise: "Whoever comes to me I will never drive away."

Jesus, You have promised that You will gladly welcome anyone who comes to You for salvation. Help me to always present that blessed message to people who need You.

HAPPY TO GIVE

"So don't be afraid, little flock. For it gives your Father great happiness to give you the Kingdom."

LUKE 12:32 NLT

In Luke 12:22–31 Jesus gave His disciples—who were, no doubt, feeling some measure of fear and anxiety over the ever-intensifying opposition and hostility they and their Master faced—a pep talk. Jesus then spoke the words in Luke 12:32 telling them not to fear, because God had happily promised to give them a place in His eternal kingdom.

Jesus directed His tender words of encouragement to His "little flock" of disciples, but it also applies to His "other sheep that are not of this sheep pen" (John 10:16 NIV), meaning others who would later follow Him and believe in Him for their salvation.

God sent Jesus into this world so you could live forever in God's eternal kingdom. And He did that happily because He *wanted* to bring you into His wonderful, everlasting presence.

Thank You, Jesus, for making a way for God to happily give me a place in His eternal kingdom.

SEEK FIRST HIS KINGDOM

"Therefore do not be anxious, saying, 'What shall we eat?' or 'What shall we drink?' or 'What shall we wear?' For the Gentiles seek after all these things, and your heavenly Father knows that you need them all. But seek first the kingdom of God and his righteousness, and all these things will be added to you."

MATTHEW 6:31–33 ESV

Life here on earth is filled with all sorts of worries and concerns. Having to care for our needs and the needs of our families can be stressful—even more so when we forget that God knows what we need and has promised to meet all our genuine needs.

In Matthew 6:31–33, Jesus invites us to lay our worries at God's feet and to "seek first the kingdom of God and his righteousness." So if you want to defeat worry and anxiety, choose to honor God every day and make His eternal kingdom your top priority.

Jesus, I choose today to seek Your kingdom above everything else and leave my earthly needs to God.

FREE IN JESUS

It is for freedom that Christ has set us free.
Stand firm, then, and do not let yourselves
be burdened again by a yoke of slavery.

GALATIANS 5:1 NIV

The apostle Paul had preached the message of salvation through faith in Jesus to people living in a place called Galatia. Paul had told them they could find forgiveness for their sins through faith in what God had done for them through Jesus' death on the cross.

Many Galatians believed Paul's message and began living for Jesus. Later, though, some Jewish religious leaders traveled from Jerusalem and convinced these Galatian Christians that they needed to add observance of the law of Moses in order to be truly saved. Paul wrote to the Galatian Christians to remind them that Jesus had died to pay the price for their sins and that they were truly free in Him.

Jesus has set you free, so stay that way! Never let anyone tell you that you must follow the law in order to be right with God.

Jesus, You are all I need to have peace with God and eternal life in heaven.

A DEEPER HEALING

And behold, some people brought to him a paralytic, lying on a bed. And when Jesus saw their faith, he said to the paralytic, "Take heart, my son; your sins are forgiven."

MATTHEW 9:2 ESV

As He so often did, Jesus shook up the Jewish religious leaders of His time when He promised to forgive the sins of a paralytic who had been brought to Him for physical healing. When some teachers of Jewish religious law heard this, they were outraged: "This fellow is blaspheming!" they said among themselves (Matthew 9:3 NIV).

These teachers were right in believing that a man who claimed the authority to forgive sins was guilty of blasphemy. What they didn't understand was that Jesus indeed had the authority to forgive sins.

Jesus healed many people of many physical problems, but His ultimate mission was to address a far greater problem: our sin. As He told those religious teachers who had accused Him of blasphemy, "The Son of Man has authority on earth to forgive sins" (Matthew 9:6 NIV).

Lord Jesus, I'm grateful that You have the authority to forgive sin, including my own sin.

FOLLOWING JESUS... INTO A STORM

Then he got into the boat and his disciples followed him. Suddenly a furious storm came up on the lake, so that the waves swept over the boat. But Jesus was sleeping.

MATTHEW 8:23–24 NIV

Jesus' disciples had no way of knowing that following Him into a boat to cross the Sea of Galilee meant encountering a storm—a furious, potentially life-threatening storm. They just chose to follow Him that day, and because they followed Him, they ended up in a place of great distress.

Imagine that! The disciples were overtaken by a violent storm *because* they followed Jesus!

Following Jesus doesn't come with a guarantee of smooth sailing in this life. In fact, there may be times when He guides us into difficulties. But when we choose to follow Him, He promises to be with us through the worst storms life brings our way.

Jesus, You never promised me an easy life as Your disciple. I choose to follow You anyway.

A BLESSING TO ALL PEOPLES

"I will bless those who bless you, and whoever curses you I will curse; and all peoples on earth will be blessed through you."

GENESIS 12:3 NIV

Adam and Eve's sin of disobedience threw humanity into chaos. But God had a plan. He would begin a race of people through whom He would eventually bring the Savior—Jesus Christ, the last Adam—into the world.

God chose a man named Abram (later called Abraham) to be the literal father of the nation of Israel. And though the people of Israel often rebelled against God, He still used this tiny nation to bless "all peoples on earth."

Many centuries later after Jesus had returned to His heavenly Father, the apostle Peter told the people of Jerusalem that the arrival of Jesus was indeed God's fulfillment of His promise to bless all nations through Abraham's family (see Acts 3:25–26).

As a Christian man, you can thank God that He has blessed you through Abraham's family—and you can also strengthen your faith by reading his story in the Bible.

Jesus, God blessed me and others who know You through Abraham's family. Thank You for keeping Your promises to him.

OVERCOMING UNBELIEF

[The father of a demon-possessed boy said,] "If you can do anything, take pity on us and help us." "'If you can'?" said Jesus. "Everything is possible for one who believes." Immediately the boy's father exclaimed, "I do believe; help me overcome my unbelief!"

Mark 9:22–24 niv

Some of the things people say in the Bible seem to invite us to get inside that person's head and see what he was really saying without actually saying it. In today's scripture passage, the father of a demon-possessed boy came to Jesus, desperately asking for help. After Jesus told him, "Everything is possible for one who believes," the father cried out, "I do believe; help me overcome my unbelief!"

That seems like a bit of a contradiction, doesn't it? But it's possible that this man knew about Jesus' miracles and was aware of the Lord's power. Perhaps the question burning in his mind was "Will Jesus provide a miracle *for me*?"

Maybe you can relate. If so, spend some time talking to Him . . .and then watch your fears and doubts melt away.

Lord Jesus, help me to believe You always, even when pangs of unbelief creep into my mind.

ACCORDING TO THE SCRIPTURES

For what I received I passed on to you as of first importance: that Christ died for our sins according to the Scriptures, that he was buried, that he was raised on the third day according to the Scriptures.

1 Corinthians 15:3–4 niv

Matthew's target audience for his Gospel was first-century Jewish Christians. The Gospel of Matthew presents Jesus as Israel's long-awaited Messiah by quoting more than sixty Old Testament prophecies and showing how Jesus fulfilled them.

In 1 Corinthians 15:3–4, Paul points out that Jesus died for our sins, was buried, and was then raised from the dead "according to the Scriptures." Paul, like Matthew, wanted his readers to understand that Jesus didn't appear in some kind of historical vacuum. Rather He was the fulfillment of dozens and dozens of Old Testament prophecies.

Some followers of Jesus choose to focus almost exclusively on the writings in the New Testament. Don't make that mistake! The Old Testament, like the New, is all about Jesus.

Thank You, Lord Jesus, for fulfilling everything the Old Testament scriptures have said about You. May I spend time reading the Old Testament so that my faith in You will be strengthened.

LOVE ALWAYS GIVES

In this the love of God was made manifest among us, that God sent his only Son into the world, so that we might live through him.

1 John 4:9 ESV

When you truly love someone, giving will always be a result. Your heart is set on meeting that person's needs and desires, even when it means personal sacrifice. The apostle John was keenly aware of God's love for him, so much so that he referred to himself several times as "the disciple Jesus loved."

John, the writer of the above scripture verse as well as the Gospel that bears his name, recorded these words from the mouth of Jesus: "For God so loved the world that he gave his one and only Son, that whoever believes in him shall not perish but have eternal life" (John 3:16 NIV).

God loves, so He gave us His very best so we could escape His judgment for our sins.

Jesus, thank You that the Father loved me so deeply that He gave the very best He has to offer: You, His one and only Son.

NOT SO WITH YOU

Jesus called them together and said, "You know that the rulers of the Gentiles lord it over them, and their high officials exercise authority over them. Not so with you. Instead, whoever wants to become great among you must be your servant, and whoever wants to be first must be your slave."

MATTHEW 20:25–27 NIV

In today's world of work, men tend to seek out more pay, more authority, and more power. Sadly, many of these "upwardly mobile" men pursue these things by climbing over or going through others.

But Jesus says that those of us who follow Him aren't to behave that way. In His kingdom, the greatest among us are those who are "others focused" and willing to serve and sacrifice for others—even at the expense of their own professional growth.

If you want to be like Jesus—and you most certainly should—then you should consider yourself a servant of others.

Jesus, You never spoke against working hard to earn promotions at work. But I know that my focus must be on serving others above everything.

A SERVANT'S ATTITUDE

[Jesus], existing in the form of God, did not consider equality with God as something to be used for His own advantage. Instead He emptied Himself by assuming the form of a slave, taking on the likeness of men. And when He had come as a man in His external form, He humbled Himself by becoming obedient to the point of death—even to death on a cross.

PHILIPPIANS 2:6–8 HCSB

The apostle Paul encouraged the Philippian Christians—and now us—toward a radical approach to their relationships with one another, namely that they should "have the same mindset as Christ Jesus" (Philippians 2:5 NIV).

In Philippians 2:6–8, Paul describes a Jesus who took "the form of a slave, taking on the likeness of men" and then "humbled Himself by becoming obedient to the point of death—even to death on a cross."

Our attitude toward others is to be like that of Jesus, whose whole focus was serving others. That's an attitude of self-denial, self-sacrifice, and unlimited giving on behalf of others.

Dear Jesus, I want to give and serve like You did. Help me to be a humble servant, just like You were.

A COMMITTED HEART

And the devil said unto him, All this power will I give thee, and the glory of them: for that is delivered unto me; and to whomsoever I will I give it. If thou therefore wilt worship me, all shall be thine.

LUKE 4:6–7 KJV

From the time He arrived on earth, Jesus knew His ultimate mission—to live a perfectly sinless life and to die on a wooden cross to pay for our sins. Everything He did and said was with an eye toward glorifying God.

The devil also knew why Jesus came to earth. And that's why he offered three temptations, all of which he cleverly designed to derail God's plan for His Son. But each time the devil tempted Jesus—and make no mistake, these were very real temptations—He answered the devil by quoting the Bible back to him (see Matthew 4:4, 7, 10). When He did that, He showed His commitment to do what His Father in heaven had sent Him to do.

We can and should be grateful that Jesus was so focused on His mission here on earth and on His commitment to the will of His Father that His heart attitude was "Not My will, but Yours be done."

Jesus, You were unshakably committed to doing the will of Your Father. Help me to remain committed to doing Your will every day.

NO CONDEMNATION

Therefore, there is now no condemnation for those who are in Christ Jesus, because through Christ Jesus the law of the Spirit who gives life has set you free from the law of sin and death.

Romans 8:1–2 niv

Many Christian men struggle with self-condemnation, believing that God holds their stumbles against them to the point that they have somehow been separated from Him. However, Romans 8:1–2 assures all followers of Christ that they aren't condemned and never will be condemned.

Without Jesus, people are lost in their sin and deserving of God's condemnation. But with Jesus, we are assured that we can't be separated from God (see Romans 8:35–39). When we feel like we could be condemned, we can look to God's promises that we can be secure in Jesus.

That's news worth sharing with people who will face condemnation if they don't repent and trust Christ as payment in full for their sins.

Lord Jesus, whenever I struggle with personal doubts, remind me that I will never be condemned because I belong to You.

ONE BODY, MANY MEMBERS

For just as each of us has one body with many members, and these members do not all have the same function, so in Christ we, though many, form one body, and each member belongs to all the others.

Romans 12:4–5 niv

The human body is a wonder of creation. It is several systems (the nervous system, the circulatory system, the digestive system, and so forth), each of which serves its own purpose. Yet all those systems are united for the one most important purpose: to keep us living and functioning as God intended.

When you were "born again," God brought you into a spiritual organism, which the apostle Paul called "one body" in Romans 12:4–5. Each member of that body—though serving different purposes within the body, though possessing very different personality traits, gifts, and skills—has been unified with others in Jesus so that we are one body in Him.

God made you the individual believer that you are. But never forget that He has also made you part of one spiritual body, the church.

Thank You, Jesus, that You have united me with other believers to form Your church.

THE WAY IT HAD TO BE

"Don't you realize that I am able right now to call to my Father, and twelve companies—more, if I want them—of fighting angels would be here, battle-ready? But if I did that, how would the Scriptures come true that say this is the way it has to be?"

MATTHEW 26:53–54 MSG

As the process of Jesus' arrest, trial, and execution began, He commanded Peter to put away his sword, telling him that at that very moment He had at His disposal thousands of battle-ready angels to come to His defense.

At that point in Jesus' earthly story, Peter and his fellow disciples still hadn't fully grasped why Jesus had come into this world in the first place. But Jesus did, and that's why He willingly faced the humiliation and agony of the coming hours.

What an amazing act of love!

Lord Jesus, You had the power and authority to put a stop to the suffering You had come to earth to face. But You were committed to the will of Your Father, who loved me enough to make the greatest sacrifice of all time.

A FAITHFUL GOD

God is faithful, who has called you into fellowship with his Son, Jesus Christ our Lord.

1 CORINTHIANS 1:9 NIV

The Bible teaches that God knew us and planned out our redemption before the foundation of the world. We who have heard and believed the message of salvation through Jesus Christ are His elect—and He promises to be faithful in keeping the many wonderful promises He has made to those who belong to Him.

God promised to send the Savior into the world (see Genesis 3:14–15), and He worked faithfully through human history to send Jesus, who came at just the right time to deliver us from the consequences of sin. He has promised that because we believed in and trusted Jesus, we will have abundant life here on earth and eternal life in a heavenly home.

Knowing all those things, we should endeavor to live lives that glorify Jesus in every way.

Lord Jesus, thank You that God is faithful, that He never changes, and that He will keep every promise He has made in You.

A LIFE MARKED BY FORGIVENESS

Get rid of all bitterness, rage, anger, harsh words, and slander, as well as all types of evil behavior. Instead, be kind to each other, tenderhearted, forgiving one another, just as God through Christ has forgiven you.

EPHESIANS 4:31–32 NLT

The church is filled with people who make mistakes, who sometimes say things they shouldn't, and who hurt and offend us. If we're not careful, the sins of bitterness, rage, anger, and others can creep into our hearts, damaging our relationships with one another and with God.

This is why the apostle Paul enjoins each of us to treat one another with kindness, to be tenderhearted toward one another, and to forgive one another, just as God has forgiven us.

Forgiveness is a huge deal to God, so huge that He sent His Son to die so we can be forgiven. And when it comes to forgiveness, He wants us to always "pay it forward" to our brothers and sisters in Christ.

Jesus, help me to always show kindness, compassion, and forgiveness to everyone, especially fellow believers. I know that when I do that, I bring glory to You and strengthen my relationship with You and others.

THE UNLIKELIEST DISCIPLE

As Jesus was walking along, he saw a man named Matthew sitting at his tax collector's booth. "Follow me and be my disciple," Jesus said to him. So Matthew got up and followed him.

MATTHEW 9:9 NLT

If any of us were starting a new movement, we wouldn't give Matthew, the writer of the Gospel that bears his name, a second look. You see, Matthew was a tax collector, which meant he was a notorious sinner who cheated the people and a collaborator with the hated Roman government.

Anybody but *this* guy, right?

There's little doubt that the Jewish citizens in Matthew's hometown of Capernaum hated him. Jesus knew about Matthew's life, yet He stepped up to his tax-collecting booth and said to him, "Follow me and be my disciple."

Matthew is an example of how a person's past, no matter how ugly it may be, does not disqualify him from following Jesus as His disciple. What Jesus calls us *to* is far more important than what He calls us *from.*

Lord Jesus, thank You that following You has nothing to do with where I was in the past and everything to do with where You want to take me, now and in the future.

HARVESTTIME

Then he said to his disciples, "The harvest is plentiful, but the laborers are few; therefore pray earnestly to the Lord of the harvest to send out laborers into his harvest."

MATTHEW 9:37–38 ESV

Have you ever walked around among a large group of people and thought about how many of them desperately need to hear the message of salvation through Jesus? God has left no doubt that we, as followers of Jesus, are to pray for those who need salvation and to speak His message to those who need to hear it.

As a follower of Jesus, you have a God-assigned purpose and plan. He wants you to act and speak in ways that glorify Him, and that includes touching the lives of others through your loving actions and through the words you speak, pointing lost sinners to the Savior who died for them.

Lord Jesus, I want to be Your laborer, one who prays and speaks Your truth in love so others can learn about You.

LOVING YOUR ENEMIES

"You have heard that it was said, 'Love your neighbor and hate your enemy.' But I tell you, love your enemies and pray for those who persecute you, that you may be children of your Father in heaven."

MATTHEW 5:43–45 NIV

Some people are not easy to love. They can be rude, demanding, surly, selfish, and unkind—even on their best days. Still others, through no fault of your own, just don't like you and treat you and speak of you negatively.

But Jesus has a message for us when we have to deal with difficult, unlovable people: love them anyway.

How we treat the unlovable, Jesus taught, reflects our relation ship with our heavenly Father. And it also shows that we understand that we are sinners saved by God's grace. We've all been selfish. We've done things that displeased God, and we've all hurt and offended others.

Yet God chooses to love us anyway, so much so that while we were still sinners, He sent Jesus to die for us.

Lord Jesus, some people are not easy to love. But I want to be like You and love them anyway.

POOR FOR OUR BENEFIT

You know the generous grace of our Lord Jesus Christ. Though he was rich, yet for your sakes he became poor, so that by his poverty he could make you rich.

2 Corinthians 8:9 NLT

Before Jesus came to earth to live as a man, He lived in eternity past as the second person of the Trinity, the Son, in the riches and grandeur of heaven. Nothing even the richest man on earth has ever enjoyed could compare.

Yet, for our sakes, Jesus chose to live on earth as a poor man. Jesus was not destitute—His Father in heaven was His provider—but He once said of Himself, "Foxes have dens and birds have nests, but the Son of Man has no place to lay his head" (Matthew 8:20 NIV).

Jesus was the perfect reflection of His Father in heaven, who demonstrated His giving, loving nature by sending His one and only Son to earth so we could know Him and live in His presence forever.

Thank You, Jesus, that You chose to leave the riches of heaven for the poverty of life on this earth so I can become eternally rich in heavenly wealth.

"WHO AM I?"

Then he asked them, "But who do you say I am?" Simon Peter answered, "You are the Messiah, the Son of the living God."

MATTHEW 16:15–16 NLT

One day Jesus asked His disciples about rumors that had been going around about Him and who He was. The twelve eagerly volunteered what they knew—that some believed He was John the Baptist, while others were saying that He was Elijah, Jeremiah, or one of the other prophets.

Jesus listened intently to the disciples' answer to His first question, and then He dropped the question He'd intended to ask them all along, the most important question in human history.

"But who do you say I am?"

Eleven of the disciples kept their mouths shut, maybe afraid they would answer incorrectly. But Peter, as he so often did, blurted out what the others may have been thinking: "You are the Messiah, the Son of the living God."

Who do you think Jesus is? That's the most important question you'll ever answer!

Father in heaven, thank You for revealing to me who Jesus really is.

OVERCOMING THE WORLD

Who is it that overcomes the world except the one who believes that Jesus is the Son of God?

1 JOHN 5:5 ESV

Shortly before He was arrested, Jesus spoke this warning/promise to His disciples: "In this world you will have trouble. But take heart! I have overcome the world" (John 16:33 NIV). This promise reflects the wonderful truth that no matter how difficult life becomes, we can live as overcomers when we abide in Jesus.

Until Jesus returns and sets all things right, the devil has free rein on this earth and in the lives of people who don't know the Lord. But the apostle John wrote that those of us who continue growing in our faith will overcome him (see 1 John 2:13–14).

First John 5:5 tells us there is but one way to overcome the world, and that is by placing our trust in Jesus, the Son of God.

Lord Jesus, this world brings me all sorts of trouble. But You have overcome the world, and that means that through You I can overcome the world as well.

LEAVING ALL FOR JESUS

What is more, I consider everything a loss because of the surpassing worth of knowing Christ Jesus my Lord, for whose sake I have lost all things. I consider them garbage, that I may gain Christ.

Philippians 3:8 niv

In the summer of 2022, Indianapolis Colts safety Khari Willis shocked the NFL world when he announced he was retiring from football to follow God's call "to devote the remainder of my life to the further advancement of the Gospel of Jesus Christ."

Willis, who gave up millions to follow God's call, can probably relate to Paul's words in Philippians 3:8. Prior to his life as the world's greatest evangelist, Paul had lived a life of great accomplishment. Yet, he considered those things "garbage" in comparison with what he gained in Jesus.

Paul is a great example for us to follow. Instead of focusing on what we've given up to follow Jesus, we should focus on what He has done for us.

Jesus, You know what I have given up to follow You. Thank You for being so much more, so much better than anything I could possibly leave behind for You.

TRUE GRATITUDE

Be thankful in all circumstances, for this is God's will for you who belong to Christ Jesus.

1 THESSALONIANS 5:18 NLT

Jesus made many wonderful promises during His earthly ministry, one of which we may sometimes wish He hadn't: "In this world you will have trouble" (John 16:33 NIV). Life in Christ here on earth isn't always easy. We will face difficulties and suffering, but today's scripture verse explains how we can not only survive but thrive when life isn't easy.

Being "thankful in all circumstances" doesn't mean we give God thanks *for* all things but *in* all things. It means that even when we are suffering, stressed out, and in serious need, we can go to God and thank Him for being in control, even when our situations seem completely out of control.

It isn't always easy to be thankful in all circumstances, but that is God's will for every person who belongs to Jesus. And because it's God's will, He will help us to do it.

Lord Jesus, when I face difficulty or suffering in this life, please remind me that it is Your will that I maintain a heart attitude of thankfulness.

BUILT UPON THE ROCK

"Everyone then who hears these words of mine and does them will be like a wise man who built his house on the rock. And the rain fell, and the floods came, and the winds blew and beat on that house, but it did not fall, because it had been founded on the rock."

Matthew 7:24–25 ESV

Jesus closed the Sermon on the Mount, the greatest sermon ever preached, with some words that both encouraged and challenged His followers to build their lives on His teaching—and by extension, on Him.

You don't have to be a master carpenter to know that a building that lasts is one that is built on a strong foundation. The same is true of our lives in Christ. If we build our lives on a weak foundation, then we're in for a life of frustration and defeat. But if our foundation is strong, we're sure to stand strong against the temptations and tests life is sure to throw our way.

Jesus, thank You for being my rock and my foundation for a life built out of faith in You.

JESUS COMPLETES WHAT HE STARTS

I am sure of this, that He who started a good work in you will carry it on to completion until the day of Christ Jesus.

PHILIPPIANS 1:6 HCSB

Many men live with the regret of failing to finish something we started. We start out with great passion and energy for what we're doing, but when the going gets tough, we lose our enthusiasm and give up.

In Philippians 1:6, Paul writes with great confidence that God always finishes what He starts by saving us through Jesus —even when the process takes much time and effort. God will never give up on you, even when you feel like giving up on yourself.

Men often feel like giving up on something because it's too hard. But nothing is too hard for God. He is more than able to grow you into the man He wants you to be, and He has promised to never give up on you.

Dear Jesus, sometimes I feel like I'm not changing fast enough, and sometimes I struggle with things I know aren't pleasing to You. Remind me daily that You have promised to finish what You have started in me.

FOLLOW HIS EXAMPLE

"For even the Son of Man did not come to be served, but to serve, and to give his life as a ransom for many."
MARK 10:45 NIV

James and John, two of Jesus' closest disciples, started quite a conflict between themselves and the other ten when they asked Jesus for a high place in His kingdom. James and John had made what can only be seen as a selfish request. But Jesus used their request to teach the twelve an important lesson—namely that they should follow His example of perfect servanthood.

Jesus is the Son of God, the King of kings and Lord of lords. But He did not come to earth to be served but to serve and to willingly give up His own life so we could live forever.

It's easy to pursue the wrong things in this life. That's why Jesus commands us to follow His example by making serving others, not seeking power and position for ourselves, our life's focus.

Lord Jesus, You set the perfect example of following God's call to serve. Help me to follow that example every day.

AN OFFENSIVE MESSAGE

Salvation is found in no one else, for there is no other name under heaven given to mankind by which we must be saved.

ACTS 4:12 NIV

If you want to offend some people, then plainly state this biblical truth: Jesus is the only path to eternal salvation. For thousands of years people have looked for meaning in life beyond the here and now—and many religious leaders have obliged them with any number of belief systems, most of which promise peace, fulfillment, and eternal bliss.

We truly live in a "whatever works for you" world, don't we?

But the apostle Peter, filled with the Holy Spirit, courageously stated the truth of the eternal life matter, telling a council of Jewish religious leaders that Jesus was the only path to eternal salvation.

Speaking the message of salvation through Jesus alone can cost you—cost you friends, family relationships, and other things that are important to you. Speak it anyway, for it is the message that sinful humans need to hear today.

Jesus, the message of salvation through You alone can be offensive to many. If I must offend anyone, let it be because I speak Your truth.

SEEKING AND SAVING

For the Son of man is come to seek and to save that which was lost.

Luke 19:10 kjv

Though it brought Jesus much criticism from Jewish religious leadership, He still made it a point to spend time with sinners. That included a wealthy tax collector named Zacchaeus, who welcomed Jesus into his home one evening.

The Jewish people of that time despised tax collectors because they worked for the Roman government and because most of them used their positions of power to swindle people. It should be no surprise, then, that Jesus was criticized for staying at Zacchaeus' home.

But Jesus wasn't just fraternizing with this sinner, and He didn't go to his home because He needed a place to stay. Jesus had come "to seek and to save that which was lost," and that included Zacchaeus.

Salvation came to the house of Zacchaeus that day, just as it continues to come to those who trust Jesus for forgiveness and salvation.

Lord Jesus, thank You for coming to earth to seek and save a lost sinner like me. Thank You for Your amazing love!

JESUS' REPRESENTATIVES

And whatever you do or say, do it as a representative of the Lord Jesus, giving thanks through him to God the Father.

COLOSSIANS 3:17 NLT

It's too easy for many men to compartmentalize our lives into the secular and the sacred—the secular being things like what we do for a living and the sacred being those things Christians do (you know, the Sunday stuff).

But today's scripture verse tells us that God wants us to be representatives of Jesus in *everything we do*. That means making sure our every action and word reflects our identities as followers of Jesus and children of the living God.

Our first thoughts each morning should be about how we can best represent Jesus in everything we do and say, knowing it's what God wants for us and what those around us need to see.

Dear Jesus, I want to be a good representative for You in everything I do and in everything I say. Help me to reflect who I am in You every day.

DENYING SELF

Jesus said to his disciples, "Whoever wants to be my disciple must deny themselves and take up their cross and follow me."

MATTHEW 16:24 NIV

Our fallen human nature recoils at the thought of denying ourselves, doesn't it? That is why Jesus' words in Matthew 16:24 can be hard to receive, and even harder to follow.

When Jesus said that His disciples were to "deny themselves and take up their cross," He was speaking of death—death to self as it is described in Galatians 5:24 (NIV): "Those who belong to Christ Jesus have crucified the flesh with its passions and desires."

Denying yourself isn't a matter of making a list of things you enjoy or desire, then drawing a line through the things you believe God wants you to give up. Rather it's a matter of giving *everything* to Jesus and following Him with your whole heart, mind, and soul.

Lord Jesus, I know You want me to live for You and not for myself. Teach me what it really means to give up my own way, take up my cross every day, and follow You without reservation.

IDENTIFYING WITH SINNERS

Jesus replied, "Let it be so now; it is proper for us to do this to fulfill all righteousness." Then John consented.

MATTHEW 3:15 NIV

Before Jesus began His earthly ministry, He approached John the Baptist at the Jordan River so He could be baptized. John's baptism was one of repentance, so he was surprised and a little confused that Jesus, the sinless Lamb of God, would make such a request.

Jesus assured John that this step was necessary to "fulfill all righteousness," so John consented and baptized Jesus. Jesus' baptism didn't fulfill all righteousness in and of itself—that wouldn't happen until He died and was raised from the dead. But it was an important step because Jesus knew He had to identify Himself with sinners—the same people He would die for about three years later.

Jesus identified with us when He was born a human, when He lived on this earth as a man, and when He died. In those ways He became one of us. And though He lived a fully sinless life, He identified with sinful humanity.

Jesus, thank You for identifying with me in every way.

A PERFECT ONE-TIME SIN SACRIFICE

Unlike those other high priests, he does not need to offer sacrifices every day. They did this for their own sins first and then for the sins of the people. But Jesus did this once for all when he offered himself as the sacrifice for the people's sins.

HEBREWS 7:27 NLT

The book of Hebrews shows its readers that Jesus is the perfect way to God, far superior to the Old Testament system of sacrifices and rituals. In Old Testament times, human priests performed animal sacrifices on behalf of the people so their sins could be forgiven. These sacrifices were only temporary solutions to an eternal problem; they had to be repeated regularly.

But Jesus' sacrifice on the cross was once-for-all, eternal, and perfect—and it never needs to be repeated. The Old Testament system of sacrifices was a mere shadow of God's perfect plan for our salvation, but Jesus is the fulfillment of that plan.

Thank You, Jesus, for willingly giving up Yourself to suffer and die as the perfect sacrifice for my sins.

MOTIVATED BY LOVE

"If you love me, obey my commandments."
JOHN 14:15 NLT

After demonstrating His love for His disciples by humbly washing their feet, Jesus issued a series of commandments: that they should follow His example by washing one another's feet (John 13:14–15), that they should love one another as He had loved them (John 13:34), and that they should put their faith in God the Father and the Son (John 14:1).

Then before promising to send the Holy Spirit, Jesus told them, "If you love me, obey my commandments." Jesus wanted them—and us today—not to be motivated by fear or the desire for God's blessing, but to be motivated by love.

The apostle John later wrote, "This is love for God: to keep his commands. And his commands are not burdensome" (1 John 5:3 NIV). If you love God, you'll do as He has commanded you.

Jesus, You have called me to obey Your commandments, not out of a sense of duty or fear but out of a heart of love for You. Help me to grow in my love for You so I can also grow in my obedience to Your commandments.

LET YOUR LIGHT SHINE!

"Neither do people light a lamp and put it under a bowl. Instead they put it on its stand, and it gives light to everyone in the house. In the same way, let your light shine before others, that they may see your good deeds and glorify your Father in heaven."

MATTHEW 5:15–16 NIV

On several occasions, the great evangelist Billy Graham posed this question: "If you were arrested for being a Christian, would there be enough evidence to convict you?" Another way to pose that question might be, in the words of Jesus, "Are you letting your light shine before others?"

Jesus is the true Light of the World (see John 8:12), and when we come to Him in faith, He fills us with His Spirit so we can grow in Him and become more and more like Him every day. When that happens, His light shines from inside us out into the world.

Jesus, You are the Light of the World. I want Your light to shine from my heart and out into the world so God will be glorified.

BORN AGAIN FOR A PURPOSE

For those whom he foreknew he also predestined to be conformed to the image of his Son, in order that he might be the firstborn among many brothers.

Romans 8:29 ESV

What is God's plan for me as a Christian man? That's an important question for us to ask ourselves, and in Romans 8:29, the apostle Paul offers a great answer, namely that each of us is to be "conformed to the image" of Jesus.

During Jesus' time on earth, He maintained His intimate relationship with God, and that allowed Him to be a perfect reflection of the character and image of His Father in heaven. In much the same way, we are to become more and more like Jesus every day as we continue our close walk with Him minute by minute, hour by hour, day by day.

Lord Jesus, I give You myself without reservation so You can work in me through the Holy Spirit to make me more and more like You every day. Please rid my life and my character of anything that does not reflect You.

JESUS' LAST WORDS FROM THE CROSS

After this, Jesus, knowing that all was now finished, said (to fulfill the Scripture), "I thirst." A jar full of sour wine stood there, so they put a sponge full of the sour wine on a hyssop branch and held it to his mouth. When Jesus had received the sour wine, he said, "It is finished," and he bowed his head and gave up his spirit.

JOHN 19:28–30 ESV

Before His arrest, Jesus prayed, "I have brought you glory on earth by finishing the work you gave me to do" (John 17:4 NIV). Jesus was just hours away from finishing that work by dying a horrific, sacrificial death on a wooden cross.

Jesus was the perfect Lamb of God who died to reconcile hopelessly lost and sinful men to God. When He cried out, "It is finished," and then breathed His last, the debt of humankind's sins was paid in full and our sins were cast forever into the deepest sea of forgetfulness (see Micah 7:19).

Dear Jesus, I owed my Creator a debt I could never pay, but You stepped in and canceled that debt for me. I can never thank You enough for what You've done for me.

KEEPING BUSY

While He was going, they were gazing into heaven, and suddenly two men in white clothes stood by them. They said, "Men of Galilee, why do you stand looking up into heaven? This Jesus, who has been taken from you into heaven, will come in the same way that you have seen Him going into heaven."

Acts 1:10–11 HCSB

As Jesus ascended back to heaven to be with His Father, His disciples looked up, frozen in amazement. Just then, two angels appeared to them and chided them for standing around, watching. It was time for the disciples to get busy, so they returned to Jerusalem, just as Jesus had commanded them.

One day, Jesus will return to earth "in the same way that [the disciples] have seen Him going into heaven." Jesus left physically, visibly, and with His disciples looking on in awe—and that's how He will return for His church. In the meantime, we should stay about the business of doing what He has called us to do.

Lord Jesus, I look forward to the day when You return. In the meantime, I will continue doing what You have called me to do.

THROUGH CHRIST'S STRENGTH

For I can do everything through
Christ, who gives me strength.
PHILIPPIANS 4:13 NLT

Nowhere in the Bible are we promised that living for the Lord would be easy. You wouldn't be wrong if you were to read God's instructions for you and then think, *I can't do it on my own!* Yet, in Philippians 4:13, the apostle Paul wrote that he could do "everything" through the strength Jesus had given him.

That's a great promise for each of us, for it means that if Jesus lives inside us, there's nothing we can't do for Him.

The next time you know God directs you to do something that seems too difficult to do in your own strength—like loving an unlovable someone or telling a friend about Jesus—don't tell yourself, "I can't!" Instead say, "I can do it through Christ, who gives me strength!"

Jesus, thank You for being with me here on earth and helping me to live, talk, and think in ways the Bible says I should. I can't do it on my own, but with You I can do everything.

TO SAVE, NOT TO CONDEMN

"For God did not send his Son into the world to condemn the world, but in order that the world might be saved through him."

JOHN 3:17 ESV

When Adam and Eve sinned, they brought death and condemnation into the world. Each man and woman born since then is under the curse of sin and death. It was the most tragic event in human history. . .but God loved humanity deeply, and He had a plan for our salvation.

When the time was right, God sent His Son, Jesus Christ, into the world not just to preach and teach a message of salvation but also to die for the sins of the world. Now we who have placed our trust in Jesus never need to fear God's eternal wrath, for "there is now no condemnation for those who are in Christ Jesus" (Romans 8:1 NIV).

This is the good news of the gospel message: Jesus wasn't sent to condemn you but to save you.

Thank You, Jesus, for coming to earth to save me. I want to speak that simple, wonderful message to others whenever I get the chance.

RECEIVING POWER

He said to them, "It is not for you to know times or periods that the Father has set by His own authority. But you will receive power when the Holy Spirit has come on you, and you will be My witnesses in Jerusalem, in all Judea and Samaria, and to the ends of the earth."

ACTS 1:7–8 HCSB

Jesus' apostles gathered around Him and asked Him what they thought was the most important remaining question: "Lord, are you at this time going to restore the kingdom to Israel?" (Acts 1:6 NIV). Instead of answering the question specifically, Jesus steered the conversation toward the mission He had planned for them—and how they would accomplish it.

Jesus told the apostles, "You will be My witnesses in Jerusalem, in all Judea and Samaria, and to the ends of the earth." He prefaced that mission statement with this promise: "You will receive power when the Holy Spirit has come on you."

Jesus knew something that the apostles would soon learn: in order to be witnesses for Him, they would need the empowerment of God's Holy Spirit. The same is true for you today!

Jesus, may I be filled with and empowered by Your Holy Spirit.

YOUR OWN MISSION FIELD

How, then, can they call on the one they have not believed in? And how can they believe in the one of whom they have not heard? And how can they hear without someone preaching to them?

ROMANS 10:14 NIV

When most of us think of the word *evangelist*, we think of great preachers standing before huge crowds of people, telling them about God's love—a love so amazing that He sent Jesus to die so our sins can be forgiven.

But, as a follower of Jesus, you are called to be His evangelist. And you don't have to stand before crowds of people or travel to Botswana, Africa, to do it. You can be an evangelist for Jesus in many, many everyday settings: having coffee with a friend, visiting with a sick relative at the hospital, inviting a neighboring family over for dinner—the settings are too many to list.

The world is your mission field, so ask God to show you opportunities to speak Jesus' wonderful name.

Jesus, help me to keep my eyes, ears, and heart in tune so I don't miss opportunities to tell others about You and Your amazing love.

INTO YOUR HANDS...

And Jesus called out with a loud voice,
"Father, into Your hands I entrust My spirit."
Saying this, He breathed His last.
Luke 23:46 hcsb

When Jesus died on the cross, it was the end of a long, torturous last several hours of a life lived to perfection. Jesus had fulfilled the law, fulfilled every prophecy, promised eternal paradise to a lost sinner who hung dying next to Him, and restored sinful humanity's broken communion with its Creator.

Jesus had carried the enormous weight of the sin of all humankind—had actually become sin for us so we, as sinners, could become the righteousness of God (see 2 Corinthians 5:21).

Once He had completed the mission for which He had come to earth—a mission He undertook for you—He yielded up His spirit to the care of His Father in heaven. Since He did those things, you get to live with Him for all eternity.

Thank You, Jesus, for doing everything You came to do.

LISTEN TO HIM!

But even as he spoke, a bright cloud overshadowed them, and a voice from the cloud said, "This is my dearly loved Son, who brings me great joy. Listen to him."

Matthew 17:5 NLT

Imagine the scene on the day of Jesus' transfiguration—the moment when Peter, James, and John saw Him in His true glory. Matthew 17:2 (NIV) reports that "his face shone like the sun, and his clothes became as white as the light." Just then, Moses and Elijah arrived on the scene.

Then came the voice of the Almighty, telling the three terrified disciples, "This is my dearly loved Son, who brings me great joy. Listen to him."

"Listen to him." That was God's clear command to Peter, James, and John—and it's His command to us today still. We are to keep listening for His voice, reading His words in the Bible—and then applying all He says.

Jesus, Your Father spoke from heaven and joyfully put His stamp of approval on everything You say. May I always listen to You and apply it.

WAITING EXPECTANTLY

He who testifies to these things says, "Surely I am coming soon." Amen. Come, Lord Jesus!

REVELATION 22:20 ESV

The book of Revelation closes with the wonderful promise of Jesus' return for His church. The apostle John had written of many disturbing visions of events that would take place on earth before Jesus' second coming.

Today's scripture verse was meant to encourage Christians to be ready and watchful for His return—whether that event takes place today, tomorrow, or years from now. We remain ready for Jesus' return when we faithfully continue (also called "abiding") our daily walk with Christ.

The Bible encourages us to long for the promise of Jesus' return, and by faith we know that will happen one day. In the meantime, Jesus gives us each day to work for Him, glorify Him, and bring others into His everlasting kingdom.

Lord Jesus, may I be found ready when You return to earth for Your church. In the meantime, I will continue to work to bring others into Your eternal kingdom.

SCRIPTURE INDEX

Old Testament

New Testament

ABOUT THE AUTHOR

Tracy M. Sumner is a freelance author, writer, and editor in Beaverton, Oregon. An avid outdoorsman, he enjoys fly-fishing on world-class Oregon waters.